D0801941

HOW TO BUY A CAR

HOW TO BUY
A CAR

A Former Car Salesman Tells All

James R. Ross

ST. MARTIN'S PRESS   *New York*

Copyright © 1980 by James R. Ross

All rights reserved. For information, write:

St. Martin's Press
175 Fifth Avenue
New York, N.Y. 10010

Manufactured in the United States of America

Library of Congress Cataloging in Publication Data

Ross, James R
    How to buy a car.

    1. Automobiles—Purchasing. I. Title.
TL162.R67   629.22'22   79-23285
ISBN 0-312-39548-5

To Shirley for her encouragement and moral support;
and to Linda for her patience and understanding.

Contents

Introduction

EACH YEAR approximately 5 percent of the nation's populace (roughly 10 million people) do battle with new-car salesmen and eventually buy a new car. Another 8 percent (about 17 million) lock horns with used-car salesmen and eventually buy a used car. Less than 10 percent of these people know exactly what they are doing and how to do it. The remaining 90 percent lose approximately $4 billion on the negotiated purchase price of the cars they buy and waste another $500 to $700 million dollars for something they usually do not receive anyway—dealer preparation. And, as if this were not bad enough, the new-car buyer/owner must sometimes live with shoddy workmanship, poor quality control, and a too-busy dealership service department that just cannot seem to find the time to correctly fix his or her car.

The used-car buyer is at the mercy of someone. Perhaps he is only at the mercy of his own set of circumstances—he cannot afford to buy a new car, or when he buys a used car he is not quite sure what to check and how to negotiate the deal. Perhaps, too, he is at the mercy of the system—a system of apathy in which no one cares whether he gets a lemon or has mechanical problems with the car—a system designed to bleed every dollar possible from his purchase.

This book was written to take you inside dealership thinking and balance the gap between what the salesman knows and uses against you, and what you know about car buying based on your own past experiences—good or bad.

The very first thing you must realize, both as the reader and as the consumer, is that there are few inflexible rules to follow when learning to buy a car. As you read, learn, and practice, you will notice similarities among all dealers and salesmen, and upon those similarities you build your car shopping and buying foundation. But aside from the truisms of the business, there are myriad variables surrounding the situation. You may scour seven different dealers and talk to as many salesmen, each with his own approach and technique. And each with his own individual bag of tricks. Strategies you successfully employ on one salesman may not work on another. So, flexibility should be your key watchword.

Author's Note. The fact that I have used the word *salesman* rather than *salesperson* throughout the book is not intended as a slight to those women who sell cars. The word *salesman* is used simply as a matter of convenience, and as a way to make this a shorter, more compact book.

HOW TO BUY A CAR

1
Choosing the Car and the Dealer

CHOOSING THE BASICS

CHOOSING MEANS selecting one from among several choices. The problems inherent in choosing are knowing what is best for you, and avoiding the myriad myths presented by salesmen anxious only for a sale. You must rely heavily on a salesman for product knowledge and advice, but you need not be completely at his mercy. Do not accept everything he says without question, for *you* are making the selection, and *you* must live with the consequences of a poor choice.

The process of choosing can be reduced to a single question: Does the function satisfy my needs? Whenever your process of selection reaches an impasse, ask this basic question: "Will it do what I need done?"

It is easy to become confused about exactly which car, with which engine in it, will be the right car for you. The best rule of thumb for the average family putting average mileage (12,000 miles per year) on its car is to avoid the smallest and the largest engines available in a given series or a given model. Make a selection from the engine(s) in the middle, provided there is a midsize offering. If you drive fewer than 12,000 miles per year, the smaller engine offers both economy and performance. If you drive more than 12,000 miles per year, the larger engine offers performance and durability.

Your personal driving habits and the use to which you put the car determine the size that is best for you. Explain to your salesman just how you plan to use the car, what economy and performance you expect, the miles you plan to drive each year, and how long you plan to keep the car. Individual needs are different and require individual consideration.

Knowing your intended use, the salesman can better counsel you according to his knowledge of the individual capabilities of the models within his product lineup. However, sometimes there is a catch. Salesmen are trained to sell what they have in stock, rather than factory order what you want or lose the sale to another dealer. Immediate sale equals immediate cash flow. When a salesman's advice seems contrary to what you ask for, test him. Does he have what you want in stock? Is he trying to sell you something only because it is all he has to offer? Will he factory order what you want? If he doesn't have what you want and is not willing to factory order it, his advice and motives are to be questioned.

Some people have preferences that will not change regardless of the arguments and logic used to dissuade them. Past experience, good or bad, will dictate their preference and choice of engine and transmission. You must avoid all myths and misconceptions based on hearsay or product misuse. Talk to people who own what you are considering and decide for yourself what is best for your needs. A car must be chosen and driven according to its limitations and capabilities.

Four Versus Six Versus Eight Cylinders. The newly introduced subcompact six-cylinder engines may pose a four-cylinder problem: too little engine for too much car. There are three basic types of six-cylinder engines: in-line six, slant six, and V-6. Each has beneficial characteristics, but the major comparison consideration is the cubic-inch displacement (CID or C.C. or liter displacement) against the body weight of the vehicle and the rated horsepower, HP. Naturally, in the same weight class, the slightly larger size offers greater longevity and better performance. Your real question is, "Will this engine pull this car for as long as that engine will?" When you have only two engine choices in a given model, take the larger, provided the engines are within 50 CID of each other. If the difference in CID is greater than 50, you should choose the smaller, otherwise you may sacrifice economy for durability that is never used. The same principle applies to four-cylinder and eight-cylinder engines—check the CID against the weight.

Diesel Versus Gasoline Engine. The major considerations here are economic: initial investment, cost of fuel, cost of maintenance, cost of repairs, and depreciated market trade value. A deisel engine is not the ideal car for a weekend backyard mechanic. It requires special tools and special knowledge to repair, which means taking it to a garage or service department after warranty expiration. And there are not that many qualified diesel mechanics around, which means you pay more for labor. The higher initial investment must be weighed against the length of ownership; in other words, will you get extra time and miles for having paid more? The lower cost of fuel and scheduled maintenance items must be brought into perspective, as must diesel durability. The projected life of a diesel is about double the life of a same-size gasoline engine pulling the same load. If you plan to buy the car and drive it until it drops, consider the diesel for longevity, if for nothing else. If you plan to keep the car for 1 or 2 years, consider the gasoline engine. The depreciated market value of the diesel vehicle cannot be accurately determined, since it will depend on market supply and demand. You must therefore assume the negative and be prepared to lose a little on trade value somewhere down the road. Finally, you are restricted in model selection, size, and style when considering the diesel. Not everyone makes a diesel car—yet.

Automatic Versus Standard Shift Transmission. You gain more economic benefits with the standard shift transmission because it gives a lower initial cost and greater fuel economy. However, some models offer only the automatic transmission, so if you favor the standard, your model selection will be restricted. The greatest advantage to the automatic is that anyone who can drive a car can drive one—no clutch, no shifting of gears. But anyone who has two functional hands and feet can learn the standard, and it only takes about a week. The cost of repairing or replacing an automatic is dramatically higher than the comparable cost for a standard shift. The trade value of the two after three years will not be that much different.

Front- Versus Rear-Wheel Drive. The benefits of pulling a car (front-wheel drive) and those of pushing a car (rear-wheel drive) are the subject of much debate. The front-wheel-drive advantages popularly sold are that front-wheel drive performs better in adverse weather (ice and snow), that there is no transmission hump running the length of the car, and that for service purposes everything is all together, right up front. The truth is that once traction breaks, front wheel drive is no better than rear wheel drive in snow and icy conditions. Front wheel drive is a more complicated drive train system and is more susceptible to malfunction than a rear wheel drive train. Front wheel drive bushings and couplings wear out faster than rear wheel drive component couplings, and are more expensive to repair or replace.

Carburetor Versus Fuel Injection. Fuel injection is more efficient and costs less to maintain and repair than a carburetor. On the same size engine (CID), choose fuel injection when you have such an option.

Other Options. Power-assisted steering is preferred primarily for ease of parking. However, most subcompacts park easily without power assist. The cost of power steering is high enough for you to consider doing without it. Test drive and park both types—with and without power assist—before you make a decision.

Rack-and-pinion steering is preferred to conventional ball-type steering for both durability and handling response. But it is not an optional choice that can be purchased, so you may have to buy a certain brand name to get it.

An overhead cam engine is preferred for longevity and performance. Like rack-and-pinion steering, it is not an option you can buy.

Be wary of component engine parts of dissimilar metals—aluminum heads with a cast-iron engine block or an aluminum engine block with cast-iron heads. Dissimilar metals contract and expand at different rates and tend to warp, crack, and malfunction. Aluminum wears out faster than cast-iron.

The Body Beautiful. Most cars are designed with a specific purpose and a specific consumer market in mind. Once the purpose has been established, the styling must be given consideration to make the car attractive enough to sell to a mass market. The major effort then becomes to design and develop a car that satisfies economy, comfort, function, and style. This is not always possible, and here is where many car shoppers and buyers meet with disappointment. For the most part, you must place your emphasis on function if you expect the greatest value per dollar invested. If the car is also pretty, all the better.

First you must select a category model: subcompact, compact, intermediate, full-size, luxury, import, station wagon, pickup, or van. Once you have selected the category, you should then compare all manufactured offerings within that category. To facilitate comparison, you must realize that there are characteristic similarities among competitive models. A compact is a compact, a full-size car is a full-size car, and so on. Your final decision should then shift emphasis from the manufacturer to function, price, individual dealership, and dealership location.

Even if you plan to keep your new car for only 2 years, project the needs of size and function over a 3-year period. You may not trade the car after 2 years as planned. If your family outgrows the car at the end of 2 years and you are stuck with the car for another year, you and your family will be uncomfortable during that third year.

Are you a one-car family? Is your new car going to be a once-a-week family-get-together car, or an everyday car? If your second car is large enough to hold the whole family, your new car can be smaller. If you are a one-car family and you need large-car roominess, buy a large car and pay extra for it; you cannot afford not to. Better a car a little too big than one too small.

How many miles per year is the car to be driven? One thousand miles per month is considered average, and for that amount of driving, any size will withstand the expected wear and tear, normal maintenance and repairs expected. The higher your mileage, the larger your car needs to be for durability and comfort.

What type of driving will be putting most of the miles on the car? Stop-and-go city driving is rougher than rigid, over-the-road driving. Even if you must sacrifice fuel economy, get the car that will withstand the rougher driving conditions. Less frequent repairs compensate for fuel economy loss.

BUYING A CAR DURING A FUEL SHORTAGE

Regardless of the exact model specification (two-door or four-door) and size best suited to your needs, fuel economy will have an effect on your final decision.

In 1973, an alleged fuel shortage sent many people to the showrooms in search of economy—anything that promised higher gas mileage and fuel savings was bought and a lot of mistakes were made. In 1974, many who impulsively bought economy cars for top dollar (no discount) traded them in on larger cars because the small car did not fit their needs and usage. Any fuel economy realized throughout the year was lost—on the initial purchase by paying full sticker price, and at trade-in time by depreciation. In 1979, another fuel shortage occurred and, again, people panicked, bought economy cars, and were soon sorry for their decision.

To be on the safe side, go back to function and usage and pick the car best suited to you in terms of size, horsepower, and special features.

Profile your "ideal" car against your first choice of economy car—price against price, feature against feature, and MPG against MPG (Miles Per Gallon). (Note: Price is the negotiated purchase price and presumes that very little discount, if any, will be found during periods of supply and demand selling.) Many midsize and full-size cars have standard equipment, such as power steering, power brakes, phonics, and radial tires, which sometimes comes as optional equipment on compacts and for which you pay extra. These costs must be considered before you can accurately analyze economy.

Each car must be compared according to its average rated MPG and according to your estimated fuel costs for 1 year. A car's average MPG is normally found on an Environmental Protection Agency (EPA) sticker found on the car itself or in a full-profile EPA booklet available at the dealership or by writing: Fuel Economy, Consumer Information Center, Pueblo, Colorado 81009. You can compute your annual fuel cost by dividing the estimated EPA rated MPG into the number of miles you expect to drive each year to get the number of gallons needed. Then multiply the quantity (gallons) times the cost per gallon. Now consider:

1. Does the cost difference justify buying a car that may not fit your needs and functional use?

2. Would you normally buy an economy car or has an alleged fuel shortage or illusion of economic crisis influenced your purchase decision?

3. Which car will perform best for you? Which will better fit your family needs and lifestyle? Which will last longest when put to your planned use?

SPECIAL CATEGORIES

Luxury Automobiles. Luxury does not always mean quality. Any luxury car, domestic or import, can have as many bugs and problems as any lower-priced car. A luxury car is built by human hands—sometimes the same hands that put together the cheaper compacts—and, in essence, has more component parts to go bad. This bothers nobody, rich or poor, as long as the car is under warranty. It is after-warranty service that will break your pocketbook if you bought the car on a shoestring. There is little mercy for the luxury car owner who is paying for service and maintenance, parts and labor. It is assumed that if you could afford the car initially, you can now afford the upkeep. Repair parts are more expensive, even though they are compatible with parts costing half as much for non-luxury cars. Tune-ups, oil changes, filters, and other maintenance items also cost more. Before you sign on the dotted line, think of the consequences you may face after the warranty expiration.

Station Wagons and Utility Vehicles. The prime consideration in choosing a station wagon or utility vehicle is function. Will it do the job that you need done? The caution to be observed is that too much power is all right, and not enough is dangerous. If the vehicle you need must haul a ton, it is all right to buy one that can haul a ton and a half; it is a waste of money to buy one designed to haul a half-ton. Pay the extra and buy the capacity you really need.

Pickups and vans at one time were easy to buy. Now you need a slide rule and a degree in engineering. Needless to say, it requires a highly skilled and knowledgeable salesman to help you decide which vehicle is best suited to your needs. Even then, you should obtain multiple opinions from several dealers to be certain the advice is the best to be found.

When considering station wagons, it is easy to get carried away with styles, colors, and amenities and end up with a wagon that does not satisfy function. Making the right choice takes a little willpower and forethought. If sacrifices must be made, always sacrifice the gingerbread items; never sacrifice function.

Imports. Import manufacturers were once the nemesis of American automakers. Economy imports now are not generally good for more than 75,000 miles of use, but then, neither are their domestic subcompact counterparts. What really sets the two apart is the cost of parts and the availability of labor for necessary repairs and maintenance. Many excellent domestic mechanics either do not want to work on imports or lack the knowledge to do so. Some import parts cost double what the comparable domestic parts cost.

Before you buy an import, pick a random service item—say, a brake job—and compare the import and domestic by calling the service departments of each respective dealer. Next, call the parts departments and compare the cost on a random part—say, a master brake cylinder. If you are prepared to live with the higher costs and you really like the import, buy it. But first consider the most common complaints of import owners.

The quality of workmanship is low, and purchase prices have skyrocketed. Critical parts are sometimes not available, and parts cost too much. The metric parts require metric tools, and self-service is often impossible because of the car's design. Trade values are low because nobody but an import dealer wants the used import on his lot; if you want a higher trade allowance you must trade your import for another import.

Brand Name Selection. People buy because other people buy. Brand-name ownership seems to run in and to affect families, coworkers, and neighbors. It is interesting to note that when one family on a given block buys a car, two or three other families on the same block will buy cars within thirty days of the first family's purchase (group contagion). Remember this when you are tempted to rush out and buy and do not know why. Did someone you know just buy a new car?

There is nothing wrong with buying under those circumstances, provided you can afford it. Never buy a car that will squeeze your budget just because someone close to you just bought. Before you take the plunge, stop and think: "Can I afford it? Do I really want it? Do I want the same type car he just bought? Do I really need it? Am I being influenced?"

The real problem with brand-name selection is that a brand name is only that: a brand name. For the most part, you will find similar service, performance, and durability in all brands. If you seriously doubt this, consider that Brand A, Brand B, and Brand C buy and sell component parts from each other. You cannot say that Brand A is better than Brand B if Brand A buys critical parts from Brand B, and vice versa. Consider, too, the industry's personnel turnover. Certain key personnel responsible for the last car that made you so happy may no longer work for the manufacturer. In fact, they may now work for the enemy who is building the car you hesitate to buy.

It is best to approach car selection with an open mind. Forget the name on the fender and let the car speak for itself.

CHOOSING A DEALER

From whom should you buy, a large dealer or a small dealer? If both offer about the same price for the same merchandise, which will take better care of you on after-sale warranty work?

Let's define small and large. A small dealer is not to be confused with a small-town dealer. Most small towns have small dealers and, in some towns, only one dealer of each particular brand name. Here, too, are found multiple-line dealers, two or three dealers who carry most of the major brand names among them. Negotiations are more difficult in a small-town atmosphere because of the element of monopoly. If it is the only movie in town, you go to it; if someone is the only dealer in town who carries the brand name you want to buy, you buy from him—at his price and on his terms.

The two major negotiating tools that may be used against the small-town dealer are time ("I'll wait until next year to buy") and competition ("If you won't give me a better deal, I'll buy Brand B"). It is difficult to shop Brand A against Brand A if the next A dealer is 60 miles away. So you must outwait the small-town dealer on price or threaten to buy Brand B.

The small dealer, by virtue of his size, has a smaller inventory from which to choose, a smaller showroom, fewer salesmen, a smaller service department, fewer mechanics, and, not surprisingly, a lower volume of business than the large dealer.

Small almost always wants to be big. While there are exceptions to the norm, most small dealers want to grow and expand their facilities. They want to increase their sales volume and someday become number one. This is accomplished by developing a clientele of happy, spread-the-good-word, repeat-business customers. Small dealers seem to appreciate your business more than larger dealers; they have not yet acquired the aloofness that often follows success and the status of being the biggest around. They may do more little favors for you than the larger dealer would under the same circumstances. But there is an opposing argument. If a dealer is small and has been small for a good number of years, perhaps there is a reason. It is possible that the small dealer has poor service, sloppy salesmen, and a care-less attitude.

However, large does not always mean better, or even adequate. The large dealer may seem better able to give you the service you need when you need it, but this is not always true. A frequent consumer complaint is that most dealers, especially large dealers, sell more cars than they can possibly service. This means that the large dealer, with a larger sales volume, could be less able to properly service every car sold.

So how do you decide? It is literally impossible to judge quality by size. Choosing a dealer usually boils down to price and reputation, which includes the reputation of the service department.

There is only one way to take the guesswork out of choosing a dealer: Talk to people who have bought from each respective dealer. Most dealers place a bumper sticker or logo label on each car they sell. When you see a car parked somewhere boasting the sticker of one of the dealers you are considering, take a few minutes to meet the owner to ask him a few questions. Do not be bashful about approaching a stranger to ask him what he thinks about his car, and about the dealer from whom he bought.

Do not restrict your investigations to one or two people, and give the small dealer the same consideration you give the large dealer—talk to the same number of people who bought from the large as bought from the small.

Do not ask a car salesman for the names of people who have bought from him. If he does give you a few names they will be those people he is 100 percent certain are happy with him, the dealership, and the car.

Check with the Better Business Bureau in your area. They can tell you much about the dealer, including the number of complaints filed against him. If there is a Consumer Protection Agency in your area, contact it. Even this does not ensure a problem-free purchase. (More on this in chapter 14, "External Recourse.")

The Automobile Broker. An automobile broker will factory order the domestic car of your choice for local delivery through the respective brand-name dealership. The automobile broker's major sales pitch is "dollars saved" (discount). You are told that he has no salesmen to pay and no facilities to maintain, and that he can sell you a new car at a little over dealer cost. Not quite so.

Working as a franchisee, the automobile broker places your order through a buying company (franchisor) who receives a fee per unit ordered. The local dealer who delivers your car receives a courtesy delivery fee of $75 to $100. The automobile broker himself will write as much profit as possible and call it a brokerage fee, a get-ready charge, a buying fee, or any combination of the three. The illusion of savings is simply that—an illusion. There are just too many fingers in the pot.

Buying through an automobile broker has intrinsic disadvantages: You cannot work a trade—you must dispose of your old car on your own; and after-the-purchase service leaves you at the mercy of a dealer who did not make a decent profit on the deal. All disadvantages of factory ordering apply to the automobile broker, for he does not carry an inventory. Inspection of merchandise is severely restricted. Your recourse is limited: the dealer made no representations—he only made the delivery—and the broker only placed an order at your request. That leaves the factory and an elusive factory representative.

2
Decision Making

WHY IS IT SO HARD?

THE HARDEST DECISION to make is the initial one to go out and buy the car. Why, then, do so many people find it so difficult to make the simple decisions about color, style, and options on the car they know they are going to buy? Several reasons seem to be true.

Pride and ego are directly involved. It is important to make the right decision in order to avoid the possibility of criticism. How will it look and how will you feel when you are showing your new car around and someone says, "Why didn't you get body side molding?" Or, "Oh, you got the four-door model; I would have bought the two-door." None of your decisions are any of their business, but some people are insensitive, and whether they mean it or not, they destroy your new-car enthusiasm. There also exists a bit of jealousy—you have a new car and they do not. To these people you need only say, "I bought this car exactly the way I wanted it; nothing more, nothing less," and let it go at that.

Fear of making the wrong decision and subsequently suffering a loss can make it difficult to reach final decisions. It is bad enough that your ego must suffer, but when you err, your pocketbook suffers as well. Any one of a dozen decisions made in error can cost you several hundred dollars. Choose a car with which you are not completely happy and you will trade it sooner than originally planned. Purchase equipment that you seldom use and you will have wasted dollars. Underload or overload the car with optional equipment and you may lose on trade value. The fear of loss can definitely hinder decision making.

If you are making an in-depth analysis of every car on the market, you

11

will eventually become thoroughly confused about what you have seen and read, what you want and do not want, and what you should buy or should not buy. Confusion is dangerous, for it inevitably leads to impulse buying. The sad consequence is that all the research and thought put into your project means nothing if you are too confused to make final decisions. You then buy the car that, for the moment, seems right for you (impulse). It is therefore best to reduce everything to writing. Trust not to memory. Utilize a system.

DECISION MAKING SYSTEMS

Comparative Analysis. To compare anything to anything, you must use the same factors throughout. This requires a firm format if you are to expect reasonably valid results for the effort. Next, your results must be gauged. You may use whatever ranges you prefer, but assigning a number value from one to ten or from one to five seems to produce the most accurate results. Areas of critical importance are measured on a scale of one to ten, and those lesser areas on a scale of one to five. Those areas of major importance will then weigh more heavily in your final average; those of lesser importance will have less effect on the total tally.

Why is it necessary to analyze, check, observe, and nitpick so many small items and so many areas of concern regarding the dealership and the salesman? The major reason is that it slows you down and forces you to think before you leap. Most purchases are emotionally inspired; you do not necessarily use logic and common sense but rather you buy because of what you touch, see, and hear. Because admen, salesmen, and marketing executives know exactly how to inspire impulse purchases, you must force yourself to avoid the influences and to *slow down*. The table on the following page will help.

If the salesman approaches you promptly, engages in polite small talk, relaxes you, and is friendly, give him a 5. If he takes his time getting to you, shows little or no interest, and does not smile, give him a 1; if he is really bad, give him a zero. If he tries to find out just what you are looking for, what you like, and what you do not like, give him a 10. If he says, "Yeh, what are you looking for? Two-door sedan? Yep, I have a few; let's take a look at them," give him a 1 or a 2. And so on down the chart. The only two exceptions will be price and location. If the dealership is 3 miles from your home, subtract 3 from 10 and rate location as 7. If it is more than 10 miles, the rating is zero. To determine a rating for price, you must begin with an arbitrary benchmark figure. It is best

Quality/Feature	Rating	Dealer					
		A	B	C	D	E	F
Approach/small talk	1–5						
Dealer's ability to discover your needs and preferences	1–10						
Presentation of product/demo ride	1–10						
Price/trade allowance	1–10						
Personality/warmth of salesman	1–5						
Total impression of salesman	1–5						
Salesman's ability to communicate	1–5						
Salesman's total product knowledge	1–5						
Dealer reputation	1–10						
Service department reputation	1–10						
Location of dealership	1–10						
Dealer's ability to meet special personal requirements	1–10						
Totals							

to use the gross profit as the benchmark (gross profit is detailed in chapter 5, "Dealer Cost"). Using a gross profit of $300, subtract 1 point from the high of 10 for each $10 over a $300 gross deal. If a dealer offers you a $330 gross deal, the rating for that deal is 7. If he offers you a $250 gross deal, the rating is 15. This puts price in perspective with all other considerations.

The same principle can be used for model selection, as follows.

Quality/Feature	Rating	Model							
		A	B	C	D	E	F	G	H
Function match to needs	1–10								
Fuel economy (EPA estimate)	1–10								
General reputation of car	1–5								
Performance/engine	1–5								
Handling/steering	1–5								
Total comfort	1–5								
Total roominess	1–5								
Styling/appearance	1–5								
Flaws/blemishes (deductions)	1–10								
Totals									

If the functional match of the car to your personal needs rates extremely high in your opinion, give it a 10. For fuel economy, pick an arbitrary figure, say 30 MPG, and add or subtract 1 point on a base value of 10 for each 1 MPG of variance. Thirty-two MPG would rate as 12; 28 MPG would rate as 8.

If you choose to use comparative analysis to reach a final decision, do not set the results aside just because they are not the results you wanted to see. You might as well save your time and not use the system if you do not abide by the final numbers.

The Balance Sheet. Salesmen use an old technique called the balance sheet to help their customers reach a decision when an impasse occurs. Here is how it works: Form two columns by drawing a line down the middle of a blank sheet of paper. At the top of one column write the word *Advantages*, and top the other column with *Disadvantages*. Then list all the advantages and disadvantages of the decision you are making under the appropriate heading. No matter how trivial or insignificant you may think an item is, list it. On another sheet of paper, make two columns with the headings *Will Use Often* and *Will Not Use Often*. Then list all options under the appropriate headings. This can be done before you begin to shop or when you sit down with a salesman. The balance sheets represent a running record of what your research has uncovered and also can be laid side by side for you to accept or reject options all at the same time. Great for avoiding confusion.

Special problem: How to Get Two or More People to Agree on a Car. Too many couples discover, after the purchase has been made, that what they bought was not really what either of them wanted. This is especially true with impulse purchases, but it applies to the supposedly well-thought-out purchase as well. You will avoid confusion and disappointment if you use a simple system called parallels prior to shopping for your next car.

To best utilize parallels, both parties must begin by keeping their wishes secret. Neither one can know the other's thinking until parallels are finally drawn. This seems to discourage communication, but if you discuss optional preferences, one side may dominate the decisions or one side may yield to the other and not express true feelings. When both can express their desires, in writing, without the intimidation of the other, an accurate picture can be drawn that leads to a final decision both can live with.

You must both follow a preset guideline of exactly what you are deciding. You can choose your color preference, but both will have to choose a color; you can pick the type interior you prefer, but both will need to pick an interior. Everything is directed toward free-will selection, but both must be making selections in the same categories for the system to work. It is therefore necessary to work from two separate lists with all options available on a given model on each list.

You now each have a list and can begin to make your selections in silence. When both lists have been completed, sit down and talk for the first time since you began. This is when you draw parallels. Compare the lists and compose a third list of all options that match on both lists. This third list describes the car with which you will both be happy.

What about items chosen that do not match up on both lists? Compromise. If you can afford everything you both want and also the options you want individually, load the car up, provided a conflict does not exist with equipment that must be one way or the other. It is impossible to have both power brakes and standard (nonpower) brakes on the same car. When you must bring the cost of the car down to an affordable level, delete first those options only one of you wants.

If parallels seems too much bother, consider the consequences: excessive shopping, arguments in front of salesmen, and constant confusion.

RESEARCH GUIDELINE

Research is very important to the decision-making process. The following sources provide information from which you can draw to make final decisions.

1. Literature from the dealer. Handouts and product information pamphlets.
2. Brief, on-the-lot inspection of merchandise before, during, or after business hours to physically acquaint you with models you may like.
3. Newspaper articles regarding particular models you like.
4. Automobile magazines—full profile information or bits and pieces.
5. Conversation with current owners of models you like, friends, neighbors, relatives, various salesmen, and other individuals within the auto industry.
6. Private garage mechanics who service most makes and models. Do not solicit generalities, but ask about a specific model or two.
7. Consumer guides, available in your local library.

If you want technical, in-depth information about a particular automobile, most dealers have product information books that contain everything you could possibly want to know about their model lineup:

specifications of the models, complete with pictures of component parts hidden from the eye—suspension, drive train, weights and measurements, gear ratios, horsepowers and torques.

When you are satisfied that you have seen enough, read enough, looked enough, and tried enough, you are ready to buy the end result of your research. How deeply you investigate and for how long are personal decisions only you can make. There are no guidelines for that.

3
Shopping

WHEN TO SHOP AND BUY

THERE IS NO BEST TIME to buy a car, but there *are* times that are better and easier than others. The consumer finds the greatest negotiating advantage at any time that business is slow. Most dealers will sacrifice more of their gross profit and allow more on trade value when their product is not selling just to do some business and keep the doors open—provided, of course, the consumer asks for the fantastic deal. Even when business is slow, a dealer will still try to make a full gross profit on the deal. When business is slow, the dealer sells fewer units and must make more money per unit just to cover fixed expenses that do not decrease in dollar amount during sales slumps. Although the dealer is more inclined to sell than you are to buy during a slump, you cannot expect a fantastic deal just for walking onto his showroom floor. It will take a little work on your part—but it will be easier.

An indicator of slow sales is the frequency with which a particular dealership runs promotional advertisements. If every day is bargain basement, deal-of-the-century day, the dealer is probably suffering for lack of business.

Your best source of information about the business climate of a particular dealership is the service department personnel. Service personnel are not trained—as the salesman is—to cover up or mislead you about how things are in general and about the dealer's sales volume. As the opportunity offers itself, saunter up to a mechanic and ask him how things are going. "How is the sales department doing? Are they selling a lot of cars?" You may acquire only a tidbit of information, but it all helps.

17

PERIODS

There are two major reasons for the automobile business to slow down: crisis periods and seasonal periods.

The Crisis Period. This is usually economic in nature, and either local or national in scope. When the general economy slumps, people tighten the belt and spend less, and those items they do buy are primarily the necessities of life. So when things are slow, take advantage of it—don't tighten your belt; spend and save.

The Seasonal Period. At certain times of the year, salesmen put forth less effort to sell to a customer and use "the fault of the season" as their excuse. All salesmen experience the seasonal slump at some time during the course of a sales year. The fact that salesmen psyche themselves out like this is a reality, and it works to your definite advantage. The following periods will give you an edge.

1. Around Christmas. This period usually runs from 2 weeks before Christmas to about 3 weeks after. During this period, a salesman's sales enthusiasm slackens as boredom sets in, and he literally becomes rusty standing around waiting for the clock to strike quitting time. To best utilize this period, you must *never* refer to the car as a Christmas present, and you must always convince the salesman that it is not that important that you buy before Christmas Eve. If the salesman suspects the car is a gift, he will hold out for a higher price.
2. Feburary. This is a small slump and most salesmen are waiting for the more active spring market to hit. Your edge is between February and spring.
3. Summer. A slight edge to be found now. It is midyear, between models, and sales are slow. Salesmen think people will be spending their money on vacations and pleasure. Play coy and act as if you can wait for the new cars to hit the market. After all, you would rather take a vacation.
4. Fall. Here there are three periods of significance: before, during, and after new-model introduction (NMI). Before NMI, the salesmen have been driven up a wall by end-of-the-year bargain hunters. The salesmen's resistance has pretty well been worn down, but they can get edgy. During NMI, salesmen become aloof—new product, excitement and enthusiasm, high profits to be made—and hold out for

top dollar on everything. About 1 month after NMI, negotiations begin to loosen up—Christmas is coming.

OTHER PERIODS

Monthly. The better times of the month are at the beginning and at the end. Most dealers project the number of units they want to sell for a given month at the beginning of that month. If they fall short of their goal toward the end of the month, they will sacrifice profit to meet their goal. Also, salesmen on a volume bonus structure will be pushing their sales managers harder to help them meet their quota. All dealers like to kick off the month well—so they write better deals during the first few selling days to get as many sales on the board as possible.

Weekly. The better times of the week follow the same pattern as those of the month—kick off well on Monday and wrap up well on Saturday. Some dealers offer their salesmen a bonus called a "Spiff" for Saturday volume. If a spiff is on, your salesman will eagerly try to see that you get the car you want at the price you want to pay. He wants volume, not profit.

Daily. You could be either too early or too late. The better time of day is from three in the afternoon onward, but not before two hours before dealership closing time. Too early in the day salesmen feel there is still plenty of time to sell someone else for more money. Past two hours before closing time and you will not have the time to employ all your strategies. When the salesman senses you are a tough sale, he will give up the effort of negotiating and appeasing just so he can go home.

Factory Strike. Do not expect to find a bargain during a factory strike. Dealers must make as much profit on their sales as possible, for they have no way of knowing when they will be able to replenish their dwindling inventories.

SHOPPING BY PHONE

A salesman is reluctant to give information by phone because he cannot show you his product, have you sign a contract, or take your money over the telephone. He is also reluctant because as soon as you have the information you need, you no longer need him. If he does not have exactly what you want, there is no reason for you to visit him and give him a chance to sell to you.

If you shop by phone, expect excuses: "I'm very busy right now; give me your name and phone number and I'll call you back in 5 minutes." Or, "I don't have my price sheet with me right now; can I have your name . . ." Be prepared to handle it in your own way. You can simply tell the salesman, that you have an unlisted number that you only give to friends and relatives. If he wants your name, give him one—real or fictitious. Stress the fact that you are indeed in the market for a car, but that you do not plan to waste time and fuel driving to his lot if he does not have what you want or if the price is too high.

To obtain information you must convince the salesman that you already have the information and are only confirming it. Make a statement and follow it with a question to get the information you want.

For example, you want a green two-door sedan. Call and say, "I saw a green two-door sedan on your lot last week and I'm interested in that car. Do you still have it or has it been sold?"

He says, "It's not here now; must have been sold."

"I heard your new pickups are selling for $8000. Is that true?"

You have a '78 you wish to trade. "I just wrecked my '78, and my insurance company only wants to give me X dollars for it as replacement value. Is that all the car is worth?" If he answers, pause, then ask, "Is that wholesale or retail value?"

You want to buy a '78. "I just wrecked my '78, and my insurance company told me to find a replacement. Do you have something similar? What do you have?"

Many salesmen will still refuse to give information regardless of your tactics, however, and will insist that you drop by for answers.

INFLUENCES ON SHOPPING

Third Party. Third-party influence comes in several assorted shapes and sizes, among which you may find your own children. The predominant third-party influence is affectionately nicknamed "the attorney."

The attorney is a friend, a neighbor, a relative who acts as your car shopping and buying spokesman. According to him, he has all of the answers, knows all about the automobile industry, is sharper than any salesman (or service manager) ever born, and can get you the deal of the century. Naturally, if you get a lousy deal or a lousy car, it will not be his fault, and no money will come from his pocket bailing you out.

You will find, on occasion, a middle-of-the-road attorney who has good intentions but just does not know enough to give excellent advice. What is really important to you is to be able to recognize the nature of the advice, how it is presented, and the individual's motives for helping you.

Bird-Dog. A bird-dog is someone who works with a salesman for a fee (a cut or a kickback) for whatever business he may bring or refer to him. Naturally, under this arrangement, the bird-dog's advice will be biased, for he has a financial interest in the matter, and you do have to buy for him to collect a dime. When you start looking for a car, treat friendly advice lightly, especially if the friend attempts to steer you toward a certain salesman. Definitely suspect his motives if he insists on personally introducing you to the salesman.

There are mechanics who will give bad advice to friends, and even relatives, because a bird-dog fee is involved. Their only concern is money in their pocket. The irony is that if the customer buys the car on the advice of his friendly mechanic and the car develops problems the mechanic should have seen originally, the customer will give him the repair work. Sweet, blind faith.

Children. Children should be seen and not heard. In fact, children should not be taken with you as you shop and negotiate. Salesmen are trained to love and win over to their side the easily influenced minds of your little angels. When the salesman succeeds at this he has a better-than-average chance of selling mom and dad, simply because of the tremendous influence children have on their parents.

Parental. When son or daughter decides to take that first big step toward independence and buy a car, problems inevitably develop. Mom and dad become overprotective, overcautious, and overbearing and want to run the show. However, most young adults know more than their parents about the merchandise and really need only financing and/or contract advice and help. Good advice to parents is this.

1. If your child likes the car, wants the car, and can afford the car, and the car checks out on the inspection and demo ride, let him have the car. It might not be the car you would buy, but it is the car he wants.
2. Do not underestimate the intelligence of your child when it comes to such worldly matters as the purchase of an automobile.
3. If you don't know what you are talking about, keep your mouth shut. You can ask questions, but you need not display your vast

knowledge. Your child knows you are smart—and the salesman couldn't care less.

4. Be an observer, and give advice only when it is solicited, or when you see something obviously amiss and detrimental that your child overlooked.

5. If your child is old enough to pay, he is old enough to play. Do not assume that just because you are cosigning for the loan that you will make all final decisions. You are only cosigning; your child must make all payments. Why should he work and pay for a car that he does not like?

ADVERTISING

Advertising, as such, is designed to draw floor traffic to the showroom where a friendly salesman can transform dreams into reality. Unfortunately, there are tricks in advertising that do more than just get you to come in and look around. Even with strict advertising codes and restrictions, the first thing a would-be offender will do is put all his brainstorm on paper and then clean it up just enough to fall within the letter of the law. Here are some of the pitfalls you should beware of.

1. *Bait and Switch Advertisement.* Bait and switch cannot be recognized by reading the ad. It must be tracked down by a personal visit to determine whether the product exists, and whether it can be bought as advertised. To bait and switch is to run a fantastic bargain-day ad with broad customer appeal. Then, when you arrive at the dealership, you are told, "You didn't respond fast enough to the ad." With bait and switch you are never "fast enough." The plan is to switch you to another car just as nice as the one advertised and, oddly enough, the only choice available. Unfortunately this one cannot be sold for the same low, low price as the one advertised. You are told, "Why not look at it while you are here? No sense making the trip in for nothing." So you look, and maybe you buy.

2. *Leader Advertisement.* A leader ad leads you into the showroom because the price is right and the model is basically what you have been thinking of buying. Unlike the bait and switch model, the car exists and can be bought at the advertised price, but it is usually a stripped-down model. If there is an equipment list in the ad, it will usually consist of standard equipment items; it looks impressive, but you could find that equipment anywhere on the same model series. So you find out that if you want more for your money you must look

at something that will cost you more. Although this is not true bait and switch, caution is advisable to avoid an impulse purchase.

3. *Monthly Payment Advertisement*. This is a direct appeal to those on a very tight budget. Suppose the best monthly payment you have been able to find on the car you want is $115 and you can afford only something around $95 a month. You would fall squarely off your rocking chair if you saw the very car you wanted advertised at a monthly payment of $91, or $24 a month less than the best deal you found thus far, and you shopped them all. Before you jump, read the fine print. A monthly payment depends upon three primary elements: the amount financed, which is derived from the purchase price less your down payment or trade-in equity; the interest rate; and the duration of the loan. If the purchase price is about the same as you found when you shopped, then the monthly payment has been made to appear lower by an increased down payment, a decreased interest rate, an increased duration of loan life, or a combination of the above. If this dealer can do it, any dealer can.

4. *Eye Catchers*. When reading advertising copy and/or literature on cars for sale, scratch out all descriptive adjectives. All words such as super, fantastic, good deal, great buy, beautiful, fully reconditioned, and so on should be removed from the ad before you decide to look at the car. These are superfluous, fill-in eye-catchers and have nothing to do with the actual quality or equipment, or the final price you will pay. The end result of this type of advertising is that you are attracted to good ad copy, rather than to the basic features of the car itself. Do not allow yourself to be influenced. Whenever you suspect advertising fraud or misrepresentation, report it to the National Advertising Review Board. (See chapter 14, "External Recourse.")

PROMOTIONALS

General. A promotion (promo) is run for one reason and one reason only—to develop floor traffic. A dealer may run a promo on five to ten cars, moderately equipped, with a special low, low price tag. The special sale price applies only to those few promo cars (limited quantity), is good only through Saturday (limited time), and is a once-in-a-lifetime offering (creates urgency to buy). The merchandise is not stripped down—it has some equipment on it—and the intention is not so much to switch the customer to another car as it is to just sell him something. The two motivating factors are price in dollars and cents, and the bargain stimulus. If these are the only two stimuli you have for going to the dealership, make them the only two conditions under which you will buy; the price must be right and it must be a valid bargain.

Limited Production. Be wary of a factory promo called New Edition, Limited Production. The styling is usually radically different from the factory's normal lineup, and "limited production" means that if it does not sell well it will be discontinued. Think twice about limited production models, for if they die on the vine, trade values die with them. You may have to keep the car until it has classic-car status before you can get a decent price for it.

Midyear Models. Watch the midyear releases. These cars will be around for a while, so you need not worry about their being discontinued. But you lose on depreciation. Even though it may be called a 76½ or a 79½, in 3 or 4 years when you are ready to trade it, the car will have depreciated back to the beginning of the model year in which it was introduced. Also, since the car is a new release, discounts will be virtually nonexistent: "If you want my new car, you must pay my price for it." You might just as well wait until the next model introduction and buy at that time.

Carryovers. The biggest promo of the year begins about two months before the models come out. "This is the time to buy," you are told. "Fantastic savings are now possible as dealers clean out their showrooms, dealers are at the mercy of the public, and no reasonable offer will be refused"—thus are announced the end-of-the-year campaigns run by dealers coast to coast.

The myth is that you can save a bundle by waiting until the last days of the model year to buy your new car. The truth is that you could have written the same deal on the same car 6 months earlier. However, if a dealer is to sell the almost 1-year-old cars he has in stock, he must make them seem like bargains. He must appeal to natural, instinctive greed. At the end of the year he is not doing you any favors; you are doing him the favor by helping him clean out his inventory.

Until the official new-model introduction (NMI), the gross profit with which a dealer has to work remains unchanged throughout the year. At NMI, his models become last year's models, acquire the name "carryovers," and acquire an extra 5 percent gross profit. This 5 percent is a factory rebate to the dealer for all carryovers delivered to retail customers after the official NMI kickoff. Consider the significance of the numbers on an $8000 car: the 5 percent rebate adds $400 to the available gross profit, which is $400 you can save by knowing it is there. Use it when negotiating on a carryover.

Demonstrators. At this time of the year the salesmen demonstrators and factory executive cars also surface to make an appeal for your dollar. The deal that can be worked on a demonstrator (demo) depends on the particular demo plan used by any given dealer, of which there are two basic forms: dealer-supplied demo and salesman-owned demo.

The tipoffs to demonstrators are the type of warranty offered and the wording of the contract placed before you. With rare exceptions, a full-term warranty offered on a salesman's demo means it is a dealer-supplied demo. If the contract to purchase states that "this is not an XYZ Dealer vehicle," it is then a salesman-owned demo, and the dealer will assume no liability whatsoever. With the dealer exempt from the contract, any recourse you need or want must come from the salesman—other than existing warranty coverage, if any.

When you deal on any demo or factory executive car, treat it as a used car as far as condition, inspection, pricing, value, and negotiations go. Dealer-supplied demos are restricted by the dealer cost percentage involved, but you do get a full factory warranty. On a salesman-owned demo, your final deal is restricted only by your ability to talk the salesman down on price. Treat a factory exec demo as you would a dealer-supplied demo, with the exception that there is an extra 5 percent with which to work (total 10 percent rebate to dealer).

When you decide to buy a dealer-supplied demo, be certain the contract to purchase states that you are to have full warranty coverage, beginning from the date of purchase and from the mileage on the car the day you take delivery.

When a dealer has no carryovers or demos in stock, you can negotiate a better deal on a brand-new car. It is no longer necessary for the dealer to create the illusion of a fantastic deal, so he can settle down and sell the new product at his normal discounts, and you can really begin to wheel and deal. With carryovers in stock, dealers go for higher profits and argue, "If you want a fantastic bargain, buy one of these carryovers. I cannot give too much discount on these brand new models." And everyone knows they can.

New-Model Introduction. For all the glitter and excitement, new car models remain, for the most part, as they were the preceding year. Occasionally the only change is a new run of serial numbers to separate last year's models from this year's (the assembly line is rarely shut down to make the transition). However, it is still a brand-new car and you want it, so the dealer has the advantage—and he will use it.

A few simple facts and rules will put you more in control of the situation. You must understand dealership thinking during new-model introduction if you plan to win and save money. Remember that:

1. The dealer must still make a profit on every car he sells.
2. He must make the carryovers seem like bargains, which means showing you a $500 difference (spread) between last year's model and this year's model (same style and equipment).
3. Holding high gross profits on the new models helps the dealer clear out his old merchandise. Bargain until he comes down to your price.
4. You can work a deal on a brand-new model as good as the end-of-the-year bargains dealers supposedly give. Write your own deal—work your own deal.
5. Determine before you walk onto the showroom whether you are going to ask to see carryover models or brand-new models, for the salesman's course of action is determined by your initial request.
6. While negotiating the deal, treat the car as if it were 6 months into the model year, rather than a brand-new item. If you mentally pretend you are buying something 6 months old, it will show in your negotiating efforts. Naturally you will not be as anxious to buy, and you will hold out more firmly for the deal you want.

4
Stock Purchase?
Factory Order?
Dealer Trade?

STOCK PURCHASE

SHOULD YOU BUY YOUR CAR from stock or factory order it? To buy from stock is to buy from a dealer's inventory; the car is there and it is yours today if you want it. To factory order is to sit down and literally build the car you want on paper; you pick the color, the interior, and only those options you want.

Dealership upper management place special emphasis and pressure upon their salesmen to get customers to buy from stock instead of factory ordering because it puts immediate profit on the books.

The major advantage to buying from stock is that you know exactly what you are buying—you can see it, feel it, and inspect it. Problems with the car can be discovered during the demonstration ride, which is something you cannot do with a factory-order car. You can delay a stock purchase or switch to another car before firm commitments are made.

Stock purchase disadvantages begin with limitations of choice; the colors, interiors, and options are restricted to what your dealers have in stock. When all dealer inventories are low, for whatever reason, you must be content to take whatever is available and hope that it is close to what you want.

Buying from stock makes you extremely vulnerable to an impulse purchase. You may become charged up emotionally, get carried away, and simply say, "Okay, write it up." A salesman will offer you a today-only deal to help you decide to buy the car: "If you come back tomorrow, it will be too late. I will not be able to give you the same deal. My sales manager wants your business today and he will bend some to get it." Don't be misled; he *will* do it tomorrow.

27

FACTORY ORDER

The greatest advantage to factory ordering is that you need not take optional equipment you do not want. On a stock purchase, to get the color and interior you want, you must take the equipment on the car as well. It is this preference that costs you extra money, and in this area alone you could save $50 to $150 on a given deal by factory ordering your car. Also, a salesman cannot utilize "Today is the only day" strategy on you. If you are willing to wait 6 weeks for delivery, you are also willing to wait until he can once again give you the price he is offering as a today-only price.

A factory order gives you time to secure a buyer for your present car. Most dealers will go along with a trade-or-sell option on the purchase contract just to make a deal. Basically, the dealer gives you a guaranteed trade-in allowance deal and a contingency deal upon the same purchase contract, which guarantees a straight cash, no-trade discount. If you sell your car, you are guaranteed the no-trade discount. If you do not sell it, the dealer will take your car in trade at a guaranteed trade-in deal price. The trick is to know which set of figures means what. It is easy for the salesman to arrange and juggle figures to make it look like you are receiving both a high trade allowance and a high discount. You must be certain that you understand whether they are collective or separate and be certain that their relationship is spelled out in black and white. How much will the car cost you, cash out of pocket, if you have a trade; and how much will the car cost if you have no trade? The difference between the two cash differences will be your trade-in allowance.

The disadvantages to factory ordering begin with delays. If you place your order and the factory goes on strike, you must wait for strike settlement before you can expect your car to be built. Since a factory strike is not your dealer's fault, the dealer would, in all probability, not be required to refund your deposit.

You cannot drive a factory-order car before you make a commitment to buy. When it arrives from the factory it bears your name, and you must take it as is, good or bad, provided it has every piece of equipment on it as ordered and is the correct color with the correct interior, or you forfeit your deposit.

You may be taken off the market by a dealer who offers you the most fantastic deal you have ever seen. This tactic is the most subtle, most damaging, and most difficult to prove of any trick a dealer might pull on you. In essence, it is a low-ball tactic. The only difference is that the normal low-ball is verbal, whereas this one is presented in writing and approved by the dealership management. You will leave the dealership convinced that you just received the proverbial deal of the century. The more you have shopped, the easier it is to be victimized. Here is how it goes:

You have shopped several dealers and have consistently been offered a deal $250 higher than you want to spend. You enter Dealer B's showroom and the salesman finds out that you want to factory order a car, that you are a shopper, and that you plan to continue to shop until you get the deal you want. He writes the deal exactly the way you want it, goes through the routine of obtaining management approval, and draws a blank. Now the fun starts. He knows he cannot give you the deal you want, so he has two options: to let you leave and take the chance that you will return, or to take you off the market right now. To do the latter, he must give you the deal you want, and so he does. You then give him a healthy deposit and think that your shopping and waiting have paid off. You go home and begin the wait. Four to 5 months later you may still be waiting for your car to arrive.

The salesman has used a twofold strategy. He has taken you off the market and he is now buying time—time for you to cool off and time for your trade-in to depreciate. His purpose is to wait and then rewrite the deal to his benefit. You will not see the car until he decides you are ready for the surprise which will normally be about 3 months later.

After 4 to 6 weeks pass, you begin to wonder where you car is, and you call the dealer. You will at first be inquisitive, then impatient, and finally hostile. You will threaten to cancel the order, ask for a deposit refund, and call the factory, and you will finally resign yourself to patiently waiting for your car. At the time of your personal resignation, progress will be observed. Now the salesman can call you with the good news: Your car is in.

When you arrive to pick up your new car, you will be told, "Prices went up, and your trade is not worth as much now as it was 4 months ago. Had your car arrived from the factory on time, we could honor the deal we originally wrote. Now we must reconstruct the deal, which begins with a fresh appraisal of your trade-in." The dealer rewrites the deal and, oddly enough, it is slightly higher than other deals you had been offered before.

Unfortunately, most victims of this tactic swallow their pride and take the new deal and the car. So what should you do if it happens to you? Refuse the car and demand full refund of all monies involved. Do not give the dealer the satisfaction of making one dime on the deal. However, it won't happen to you if you take a few precautions.

Be certain there is an automatic time-cancellation clause within the factory-order purchase contract. If the car is not delivered to you on or before a certain date, you will automatically have the right to cancel the order with a full refund of your deposit—no questions asked. This protects you against the delaying tactic of an unscrupulous dealer, and against factory workers' strikes delaying delivery. Word the clause informally and allow a reasonable length of time for dealer performance—about 6 to 8 weeks.

One week before the deadline date, find a back-up car to buy if for any reason your factory order deal falls apart. If you have a back-up car located, you will be less tempted to take the factory order if the dealer raises the price.

DEALER TRADE

Dealer trading involves your dealer's (A) contacting another dealer (B) who has a car in stock just the way you want it. Dealer A then either trades one of his cars in stock for the car he wants from Dealer B or he buys the car outright from B to sell to you. Dealer A acquires the car and delivers it to you from his lot. Trading gives you the advantages of a factory-order car without the time delay and avoids the disadvantages of shopping.

How does your dealer know just what is available from every other dealer? He has a coded master book that shows him who has what and when they got it. Some use microfilm and can scan for your car in minutes. The real question is not whether your dealer *can* do it but whether he *will* do it. The two basic reasons he would not are that it is time-consuming—double the paperwork—and that it becomes obligatory to return the favor.

Buy from stock? Factory order? Dealer trade? Give the choices very serious thought before you make a commitment.

5
Dealer Cost

A GOOD DEAL is a state of mind, an attitude. What seems lousy to one seems excellent to another. Some people shop a dozen dealers and never know when enough is enough, and they never recognize a true bargain when they find one. Others shop two dealers, take the lower of the two prices, and consider themselves fortunate. If you are happy with the salesman, the dealership, and the figures you receive, you have found a good deal, even if another dealer might go slightly lower on price and higher on trade value.

A good deal to some is simply a car that their budget can afford. Never feel that a deal is good just because it is affordable.

DEALER COST

Your knowing dealer cost and the way to work a deal does not automatically guarantee performance and cooperation on the part of the salesman and dealership management. What it does do is give you a benchmark from which to begin negotiations. It tells you how much room a salesman has to move on a given deal and eliminates many of the last-moment surprises when the ink hits the paper.

Dealer cost, simply stated, is the cost to the dealer for his merchandise. Cost includes not only the charge for the product, but also all expenses incurred by the dealer before the vehicle is finally sold to the end user, such as the fuel put into the gas tank at the factory, the antifreeze in the cooling system, any advertising charges levied against the dealer by the factory, and the interest paid to a lending institution under floor planning (a system of borrowing and repaying money on a dealer's inventory for a fee).

Because of these variables, it is literally impossible to compute pure dealer cost on any given car without having access to the dealer's books. The percent factor is different from model to model, so dealer cost becomes a conditional figure. The best you can ever hope to compute is a practical, functional figure that will permit you to negotiate your deal anywhere. Functional cost percentages are used by salesmen and sales managers alike to do a deal workup, unless they are working an extremely low gross profit deal, at which time they would go to a cost book for a to-the-penny cost on a particular car.

The percent factor used to compute functional dealer cost follows model designation. For domestic automobiles the percent factor is as follows:

- Subcompacts   10 percent

- Compacts   13 percent

- Intermediates   17 percent

- Full-size   21 percent

- Luxury Full-size   21 percent

- Pick-ups and Vans   20 percent

For import automobiles the percent factor is as follows:

- Subcompacts   9 percent

- Compacts   10 percent

- Pick-ups   13 percent

- Luxury imports   16 percent

Floor Planning. A floor plan charge is a fixed percentage computed against the dealer's cost on each car he has in stock. This percentage usually follows prime rate and may therefore vary from time to time. For all practical purposes the percentage you use is three-quarters of 1 percent (.0075). When a dealer receives his merchandise he notifies the lendor, the lendor pays the factory, and the floor plan charge begins to accumulate. When the car is sold, the dealer notifies the lendor and either pays the balance on that car or, if the car is financed on dealer paper (see chapter 12, "Financing"), sends the paper to the lendor to stop the floor plan charge.

Most people believe that the longer a car sits on a dealer's lot the better the deal should be; the dealer should give a larger discount or sacrifice some profit for the sake of getting rid of the car. Quite the contrary is true. The longer the car sits, the more money the dealer has invested, so the higher the price. It is possible to work a $100-better deal between two identically priced cars provided you know about how long they have been in a dealer's inventory.

Most cars have a plate somewhere on the body that gives the month and year of manufacture. The plate will be just inside the doorjamb on the driver's side, or on the firewall or wheel well inside the engine compartment. The lag between date of manufacture and date of delivery is small, for the factory wants the money for the car as soon as possible. If the plate shows November and it is now March, it is safe to assume the car has been on the dealer's lot 4 months. Cost times .0075 per month times 4 months equals floor plan charge.

COST COMPUTATIONS

The percentages you now have can be utilized in two ways: to compute available gross profit, and to compute functional dealer cost (cost). For example, to compute the gross profit on a compact with a sticker price of $4,000, multiply 13 percent by $4,000, which will yield a $520 gross profit. From this $520 must come the floor plan and dealer's profit. To compute cost on the same car, simply subtract the $520 from the sticker price or use a percent multiple. To derive a percent multiple, subtract the 13 percent factor from 100 percent, which yields 87 percent. Multiply 87 percent by the sticker price for a cost of $3,480. A 17 percent gross profit factor will yield an 83 percent cost factor, and so on.

Gross profit and cost computations can be utilized in three ways:
1. Straight, no-trade deal working from dealer cost and adding profit.
2. Straight, no-trade deal using gross profit to discount the sticker price.
3. Trade-involved deal using gross profit to pack the trade.

Various circumstances dictate the use of one method over another, although adding or subtracting will eventually give the same answer.

Dealer cost is generally used on a straight, no-trade deal first computing the actual cost of the car and then negotiating upward. The floor plan charge must be added to cost before you can begin to negotiate.

Gross profit must be used when a trade is involved. It is necessary to know exactly how far down the price can be taken and still have some left for dealer profit. Knowing dealer cost tells you that much but, with a trade, the play money (gross within the car) is used to pack the trade valuation. You must know just how much is available for packing, and how much is left after packing is done. When you are in a situation involving a split deal that uses part of the gross to pack the trade and shows part of it as a discount, it becomes very confusing if you do not know the total gross available.

Here are the dealer cost computations on an $8,000 compact, intermediate, and full-size car set side by side.

Compact	*Intermediate*	*Full-Size*
$8,000 Sticker price	$8,000 Sticker price	$8,000 Sticker
× .87 Factor	× .83 Factor	× .79 Factor
$6,960 Cost	$6,640 Cost	$6,320 Cost

Next, compute and add floor plan if applicable. Assume these cars have been in stock for 3 months. Each would then have .75 percent computed against it per month:

$6,960	Cost	$6,640	Cost		$6,320
× .0075	Floor plan factor	× .0075	Floor plan factor	×	.0075
$52.20	per month	$49.80	Per month		$47.40
× 3	Months	× 3	Months	×	3
$156.60	Floor plan charge	$149.40	Floor plan charge		$142.20

Add the floor plan charge to the cost figure and negotiate up until the dealer says, "Okay, I'll take the deal," or until you have gone as far as you care to go. Once the benchmark has been established, any offer you make over that amount is profit for the dealer. It is then merely a question of how much profit he wants to make and how high you want to go on price.

When you have a trade-in it becomes a bit more difficult. Follow this example using a $7,000 compact as the car you want to buy, and a theoretical wholesale value on your trade-in of $2,000. A salesman may show it like this:

$7000 Sticker price
−$2410 Trade allowance
$4590 Cash difference

How did he get $2,410 for a trade allowance? Your trade is worth only $2,000. Why didn't you receive a discount?

Using a 13 percent factor to compute functional gross, the dealer has $910 with which to work. Initially he tries to make a $500 gross profit deal and adds $410 of his gross to your trade value to increase it to $2,410. If you negotiate, he will move up in $25 to $50 increments until he has consumed another $100, at which point he will show you a $2,510 trade allowance and a cash difference of $4,490. The only thing that has really changed is the amount of profit he is willing to accept. Your trade is still worth only $2,000.

Suppose that halfway through the negotiations you decide to switch to an intermediate. What then?

The salesman recomputes his opening deal according to the new markup percent. He uses the same trade value—$2,000—but now he has an extra 4 percent to utilize. His available gross is now $1,190; he may offer you $2,690 for your trade, which will yield a cash difference of $4,310, and a profit of $500. Even if you had already negotiated him down to a $200 gross profit deal on the compact, the dealer will use your switch to an intermediate to go back up to a high gross. On a full-size car he can make things look better and make more money. Placed side by side, the deals look like this:

Compact	Intermediate	Full-Size
$7,000 Sticker price	$7,000 Sticker price	$7,000 Sticker price
× .13 Factor	× .17 Factor	× .21 Factor
$910 Gross profit	$1,190 Gross profit	$1,470 Gross profit

To hold a $500 profit on each deal written against your trade, the pack is:

$410 Compact	$690 Intermediate	$970 Full-Size

Which gives you a revised trade allowance of:

$2,000 Wholesale	$2,000 Wholesale	$2,000 Wholesale
+ $ 410 Pack	+ $ 690 Pack	+ $ 970 Pack
$2,410 Trade allowance	$2,690 Trade allowance	$2,970 Trade allowance

The cash difference becomes:

$7,000 Sticker price	$7,000 Sticker price	$7,000 Sticker price
− $2,410 Allowance	− $2,690 Allowance	− $2,970 Allowance
$4,590 Cash difference	$4,310 Cash difference	$4,030 Cash difference

Note that the real value of your trade and the profit held did not change during the computations. If the salesman wants to confuse the issue, he can split the deal and show a trade allowance and a discount. This is usually done on cars with high grosses. The trick is to show you what seems to be retail for your trade and still give a discount on top of it all. Retail on your car should be about $2,600 (wholesale plus a $600 spread), using a $2,000 trade value and a $7,000 full-size car; gross profit to play with is $1,490.

$2,400 Trade allowance	$7,000 Sticker price
+ $ 200 Over allowance	− $ 300 Discount
$2,600 Total allowance	$6,700 Discounted price
	− $2,600 Total allowance on trade
	$4,100 Cash difference

All of which says the dealer will make a $590 gross profit on this deal if you accept it. Breakdown: The salesman could have shown you a total allowance of $2,900 and derived the same cash difference, but psychologically you would not be as content nor as set up if you saw everything in lump sum. The more he breaks the figures down, the more it seems he is giving. When the salesman offers both a trade figure and a discount, it seems as if you are receiving more than the average customer. Additionally, the dealer has shown you an overallowance on your trade. If you ask for more he will point to the extra $200 and tell you that he has surpassed your car's value as it is; he can go no further. Now it seems the only area left for you to negotiate is the discount. Even there he will fall back upon the fact that nobody gives a discount when a trade is involved. What can you say?

Forget the trade allowance, the overallowance, and the discount and concentrate on the cash difference. Any reference you make to what he has given you thus far is really wasted breath. What is the bottom-line figure? Compute the deal you want based on the gross available and the wholesale value of your car. If the cash differences match, buy the car. If they do not match, then attack the cash difference figure the salesman is quoting.

If one tactic does not work, a salesman will take a different approach. If he cannot grab you by switching or splitting the deal, he will try to nail you on cash difference or monthly payment. In the final analysis it is the bottomline that counts—just how much will the car cost you in dollars and cents?

If a deal does not have enough gross for the salesman to wheel and deal, he may create his own gross. The easiest way is for him to pack (misquote) the sticker price. This is done primarily on factory-order cars and used cars. The salesman may also pack the adding machine, which produces supportive evidence that the price he is quoting is true. A salesman punches the pack (say $200) into the adding machine and, without clearing the machine, tears the tape off. Thereafter, whatever calculations are done on the machine produce a bottom-line figure $200 higher than should be. When a salesman itemizes your options on a tape, you will look at the list and assume that the total is a true and accurate price.

Your best defense is to double-check the prices quoted for options and the base price of the car you plan to buy. These can be checked against the dealer's book and against window stickers on cars already on his lot. Double-check arithmetic personally, either with a pocket calculator or by long-hand addition.

PROFIT LEVELS

Most dealers within a given size hold a certain profit level. There are exceptions, but you do not want to spend 6 months finding an exception. You can go to as few as two dealers and find the deal you want; conversely, you can go to as many as a dozen dealers and not find that much difference between the valid deals you can work and obtain.

Here are the various profit levels held by most dealers:

No discount Car is sold for full sticker price. If a trade is involved, the wholesale value is allowed; no gross is used for packing.

$500 and higher Factory order; intermediates and full-size cars; used cars; trucks and vans—new and used.

$400 to $500	Borderline on factory order on intermediates and full-size cars; out-of-stock purchases. Normal, average dealer range.
$350 and up	Guaranteed deal on any car. Dealer may try for more profit, but when he is this close to a deal, he will push very little.
$300 to $350	Negotiating level. Slow market will make dealing easier.
$200 to $300	Strong negotiating necessary; make two or three trips to dealership to obtain acceptance of a $200 gross deal.
$100 to $200	Fleet sales; multiple purchase of three or more; promos.
$ 50 to $100	Dealer promo; demo sales; leader ads; extremely slow market.

These guidelines are not rigid but they do give you an idea of what to expect under certain circumstances. Knowledge is savings.

What May Happen. The easiest way for a salesman to offset your knowledge of dealer cost is to deny that both your knowledge and your figures exist. The logic is that if he says something long enough and loud enough you will begin to believe it, accept it, and act upon it. His story may go like this:

"So many people knew cost that the factory restructured the percentages. We do not have half the money available that we had in the past. The figures you have would have been good last year, but not anymore." With this statement, the salesman confuses you, creates doubt and, for the most part, captures the negotiating advantage. You are not fully certain that he is telling you the truth, and that slight doubt begins to weigh on your mind and has a direct effect on your final decisions. If you ask, "Just how much will the car cost under the new system?" you are nibbling his bait. He then pulls the line by quoting you a best-deal-in-town price. He will begin by assuring you that while your figures are wrong, you are not that far off. "Here is what I can do for you, and it is not far from what you had in mind."

Your best defense against this maneuver is to use the "other dealer approach.'' Simply tell the salesman that another dealer must still be using the old set of figures (percentages), because he will give you the car you want at the price you want to pay. ''If he can do it, why can't you?'' Back this up with, ''Naturally I would rather buy from your dealership, but price is important.''

A salesman may try to convince you that the maximum discount he can give is a fleet discount, which is only 6 percent to 7 percent of sticker price. This, he will assure you, is the discount normally reserved for fleet customers only, and you will be lucky indeed if he can talk his sales manager into giving you that much. Question his discount: ''If 7 percent is the best you can do, why can the dealer down the street do better?'' Or, ''If you give only 7 percent to your fleet accounts, why do they continue to buy from you? Other dealers give much more to the general public, and I am sure they do better for their fleet accounts.''

The dealer may advertise copies of so-called factory invoices in the newspapers showing a below-invoice price to you after the discount, or advertise factory invoice disclosure upon personal visit to his showroom and personal request, or show you phony factory invoices prepared by his secretary and passed off as authentic. These phony invoices look real enough, but they generally carry a $200 to $400 pack. No dealer anywhere will sell his product at a loss (below his cost), so do not be misled for a moment. Disregard the ad, and disregard the dealer completely. If he uses this ploy in any form, he is not to be trusted in any other area—service, reliability, or financing. The only way at all that he can sell a new car below invoice without losing money is to sell a used new car, a repossession, a factory exec's car, or a demonstrator—all of which may or may not show the true mileage and carry a full factory warranty.

The real confusion about the cost factor is to be found on compacts that approach intermediate size. Unless the salesman tells you it is a compact, you may become confused by size alone and utilize a 17 percent factor— 4 percent too high for a compact. You will then be negotiating below dealer cost.

If you are in doubt about a cost factor, you will find the answer you need in one of several publications released each year that give dealer cost on any given make and model of new car. These paperbacks can normally be found at most bookstores and at some drugstore book racks. When in doubt, check it out. When you find the dealer cost you need to know, divide that amount by the retail price of the car and you will have your cost factor percentage.

6
Your Old Car Is Worth More Than You Think

GETTING READY

UNLESS YOUR CAR needs body work (it has rust or crash damage), if it has no obvious defects, you can put it in A-1 trade-in shape for less than $50. First and foremost, it must be clean from bumper to bumper—every piece of dirt and dust detracts from its value. The engine compartment is the kicker, for any car will develop dirt on the engine after a few years' use. If your engine is throwing or leaking a little oil, the oil will capture dirt and build a thick layer of goop, making the car look like junkyard material. It costs a lot to have an engine steam-cleaned, but you can do as well at a local spray-jet car wash. Use plastic wrap to completely cover the distributor and alternator before you spray to avoid forcing greasy water into critical electrical parts. Then soap-spray the entire engine and all exposed metal within the engine compartment. Rinse with clear water and you have an engine that looks about the same as when you first bought the car. Clean out the trunk and glove box, leaving the spare tire and jack in the trunk and the owner's manual in the glove box.

Cover, repair, or replace all blemishes on your car. Tape small cuts, tears, or holes in upholstery with matching color rubberized or vinyl tape. Cover blemishes on quarter panels and rocker panels with a quick coat of spray paint (it doesn't have to be a perfect job). Make a vinyl top look new with vinyl spray paint (relatively inexpensive and it comes in colors). You are now psychologically ready to ask top dollar for your car.

When you determine trade value, be fair about it. You must put yourself in the other person's shoes and view the car as he does. As the buyer, would you pay cash-out-of-pocket today what you think your car is worth, or would you try to chop the price by picking the car apart? When you have been to several dealers and all seem to be close on the trade value offered, perhaps an adjustment is necessary in your figures. Be flexible.

You must realize three truisms:

1. Your car is worth only X number of dollars—period.
2. There are only X number of dollars of gross profit available on a given car.
3. A dealer must make a profit on each and every car he sells.

Do not expect full retail allowance for the unused portion of recent repairs and replacement items you have purchased. The dealer does not care how long ago a replacement or repair was made as long as the parts are functional now. He could care less if there are 33 months left on the battery, 30,000 miles left on the tires, and 20 months left on the muffler.

At best, recent repairs and replacement items will give you a little negotiating leverage: "My car will sell for you faster; it will cost you less to fix."

THE APPRAISAL

Dealers use many methods to appraise a car. These methods depend on how the deal is first put together, who makes the intitial move, and who makes the initial dollar offer to whom. The major categories of appraisal are:

1. The salesman inspects the car subject to management approval and does a rough deal workup from his inspection.
2. The sales manager inspects and appraises the car and does a workup offer that the salesman presents to the customer, or the sales manager appraises the car after a workup done by the salesman.
3. A professional appraiser inspects the car, sets a value on it, and gives this figure either to the salesman or to the sales manager to begin a workup. He sets an inflexible value upon your car that nobody (salesman or sales manager) goes above, no matter what. It is always a wholesale figure.

A salesman is taught to inspect your trade-in in silence, while you watch. He will touch blemishes on your trade without saying a word, but he will be sure you see him touch them. This lets you know that he knows the blemish is there without verbally offending you. As he silently lets you know just how much is wrong with your car, your mental value of it diminishes. He is setting you up for final negotiations.

When a salesman says, "Let's take a look at your car," let him go alone. Go over and look at his car again or wander around the lot. If he calls you over to ask you a question, answer the question and wander away again while he continues his visual inspection of your car. If he insists that you stand by while he inspects, tell him you must make a telephone call, or tell him you want to inspect his merchandise, and that there is no real reason that you can see for you to stand around while he looks at a car that you see every day. This ruins his little game and will leave you free to ask for top dollar when you sit down to negotiate the deal.

The inspection is an area in which you can gain a definite advantage over the salesman. He must stand by as you inspect his merchandise, but you need not stand by while he inspects yours. You can do it to him, but he cannot do it to you if you walk away.

Another common ploy to diminish your trade value is to talk your trade down. Since it might offend you to talk about your particular car, most salesmen will third-party your trade by talking about other cars just like yours: how bad they are; what bad luck they have had selling them; how low the value is; and the fact that there is an overabundance of that particular model on all used-car lots just now. Sometimes this is true. Even so, no matter what the story, no matter what the offer to you, you always have the right to negotiate, to make a counteroffer, and to leave and shop elsewhere. Write your own deal, make him an offer, and put the ball in his lap.

After a salesman performs an inspection, he may do a deal workup and make you an offer, or he may try to get you to make a commitment on exactly how much it will take to make you buy. Regardless of who makes the commitment—salesman or customer—final papers must be drawn to bind the deal and make it official. These papers may be called a workup sheet, a specification sheet, an agreement to purchase, or a contract, but the common elements are that the terms are set forth in print, and you must sign on the dotted line. The papers, with deposit, are taken to the sales manager for appraisal and approval or counteroffer. Because the deal is subject to management approval, all the salesman is telling you is that he will try to get the trade allowance on which the two of you have come to terms. There is no commitment on his part, although you must make a commitment to purchase at that price.

The sales manager's appraisal of your car may come after the salesman's inspection and completion of the workup sheet, or it may be used as an entirely different method of handling you. In the first instance, the sales manager will look over the deal as written and then appraise your car and set a trade value from which the final deal will be drawn. The salesman must then reenter the closing room with either an approved deal, as mutually agreed upon, or a counteroffer to present for your approval. In the latter case, when you ask the salesman how much your car is worth, he will have his sales manager perform an appraisal on your car. The sales manager will give the salesman an offer to present to you. The salesman must then sell you the deal his sales manager has written.

For the most part, the advantages of the latter favor the customer; you make no commitment to buy, whether or not the figures are exactly what you want. You have the option to review the deal and accept it or reject it and leave. Why then would a dealer choose this method of appraisal approach?

Even though most of the benefits favor the customer, the dealer gets one major benefit, and it can cost you money. Psychologically, you will feel that this is the best the dealer will do on trade value, and you further believe that since the sales manager did the appraisal, it will do little good to argue with the salesman for a higher allowance. If you do object to the deal the salesman can always stop you from leaving by saying, "Wait a minute. Let me see if my sales manager will go a little higher on your allowance." And so the negotiations begin—offers and counteroffers—until everyone is happy.

Precaution. When a salesman asks for the keys to your car for an appraisal, do not let the keys or the car out of your sight. If the salesman, his sales manager, or a professional appraiser wants to take your car for a ride to check it out—go with him. Any time you are away from your car, have the keys in your pocket. There are three major reasons for this:

1. You want to know where your car is taken. If it is shopped to a wholesaler or a used-car lot, you can expect a very low trade allowance. If the dealer drives it around the block, you know he plans to keep the car for resale.
2. You want to know the dealer or appraiser is not going to hot-rod, sabotage, or otherwise abuse your car while inspecting it.
3. You want to know where your car is finally parked. Some dealers hide the trade-in or keep the keys to coerce the customer to "go ahead and buy" their car. If they feel they are not going to get the sale anyway, they have little to lose by harassing you. It is best to have an expendable set of keys made before you begin to shop. If

someone doesn't want to return your keys, tell him to keep them, get in your car, and leave.

SOURCES OF TRADE VALUE

Even though you will be able to determine trade value by depreciation (computations later in this chapter), it will be worthwhile to average trade value by using one or more of the following sources:

1. Used-car dealer. Direct purchase of your car. Take your car to a used-car dealer and ask him how much he will give you for it today on an outright purchase—no trade, no dickering on price. When he quotes a figure (it will be wholesale), tell him you will think about it and leave.
2. New-car dealer. Same procedure as for the used-car dealer. The figure will be wholesale or less.
3. Used-car ads. New- and used-car dealers and private owners advertising their cars for sale. This will be a retail figure.
4. Wholesale and retail guide books; blue-book value when you have access to the information. You want the wholesale value of your car.
5. Banks, credit unions, loan companies, and insurance companies. They may or may not be willing to give information. You want the wholesale value.

When you have all figures from outside sources, convert the retail to wholesale by subtracting $600 ($1,000 for luxury cars), and add all figures together. Divide that sum by the total number of figures you have added. This gives you an average wholesale profile value based on current market conditions. Add this figure to the depreciated value figure, divide by 2, and you have a sum total average of what your car should bring on the open market.

VALUE BY DEPRECIATION

All cars depreciate at approximately the same rate as their percent of markup. (Refer to dealer cost factors, page 34.) When you buy and drive a new car off the lot, it depreciates down to dealer cost less 10 percent, which is the first-year depreciation. For example, you just bought a new $7,000 sticker-priced, full-size car; 79 percent factor (see page 34). It is worth dealer cost ($5,530) less 10 percent ($553), or $4,977. To determine true value (wholesale), deduct $600, and the value of your new car is $4,377, or about $4,400. To go into second-year devaluation, take 79 percent of $4,977, which yields $3,931 ($3,900 to round it off) for the retail valuation of your car in its second year. The 10 percent is deducted only in the first year. Subtract $600 from $3,900 and the wholesale value of your car at age two is $3,300. If you have a 5-year-old model car, you would use the current sticker price of a brand-new model X and depreciate that down 5 years. The following tables will help eliminate confusion about computing value:

	Full-Size Car	Intermediate Car	Compact Car	SubCompact Car
Sticker Price	$7,500	$6,500	$5,500	$4,500
Cost Factor	× .79	× .83	× .87	× .90
Dealer Cost	$5,925	$5,395	$4,785	$4,050
Less 10 Percent	× .90	× .90	× .90	× .90
Retail First Year	$5,333	$4,856	$4,307	$3,645
	$5,333	$4,856	$4,307	$3,645
	× .79	× .83	× .87	× .90
Retail Second Year	$4,213	$4,030	$3,747	$3,280
	$4,213	$4,030	$3,747	$3,280
	× .79	× .83	× .87	× .90
Retail Third Year	$3,328	$3,345	$3,260	$2,952

To compute the retail value of your trade-in, run your computations out as above to the age of your car. If it is 4 months into the model year (model year beginning in September), compute the next year (a 5-year-old car would run to the sixth year retail), and subtract the sixth-year figure from the fifth-year figure. This will give you the total depreciation between year 5 and year 6. Divide the difference by 12 to obtain the average depreciation per month for that full year. Multiply that figure by the number of months you are into the model year. Subtract that figure from the retail value fifth year and you will have the current retail value of your car.

Retail Fifth Year: $2,076
Retail Sixth Year: $1,640 depreciation from fifth year to sixth year

The depreciation per month (rounded off) is $436 divided by 12, or $36. Thirty-six dollars per month times 4 months equals $144 depreciation for

4 months. Retail fifth year, less $144, equals true retail value, current . . . $1,832. Wholesale fifth (4 months into model year) $1832 less $600 ($1,000 for luxury cars) yields a computed wholesale value of $1,232. Match this figure against market profile, and with the resulting figure begin to work your deal.

7
Trade It or Sell It?

WHY NOT TRADE?

YOU SHOULD HAVE A GOOD IDEA before you begin to shop whether you want to trade your car or want to sell it yourself. Selling your car represents a savings to you (dollars in pocket), but trading represents convenience. You need not run advertisements in the paper, answer phone calls, show your car to every shopper in town, listen to complaints and criticisms, or negotiate with prospective buyers.

Most people prefer the convenience of driving in with the old car and driving out with the new. It may take several months to sell your car on your own, but it could sell with the first phone call you receive. Because you may not find exactly what you want when your car sells, you may have to accept second best. Also, the sale of your car creates an urgent desire to replace it, which makes you subject to an impulse purchase and vulnerable to a poor deal.

If you can live without your car for a short period of time, at least make the effort to find a buyer. If yours is a one-car family, make the sale of your car contingent upon the purchase of your new car. Put a time limit for performance within the agreement to purchase, take a deposit of good faith from your buyer, and start looking for the car and the deal you want. If a buyer is serious enough about buying your car, he will not mind if the delivery is delayed 2 or 3 days while you consummate your purchase. Naturally, the deposit is returned if your new-car plans fall apart.

SELLING YOUR CAR

It will be necessary to place a realistic price tag on your car if you expect a quick sale. Remember, every dealer in town is in competition with you to sell your potential customer a car just like yours. You must therefore be competitive in both price and quality. Determine what dealers are doing in the marketplace, and make your quotes slightly less to draw customer traffic. From there you can negotiate price right down to wholesale—something the average dealer will not do. Why sell for wholesale if a dealer will allow you wholesale for your car? Why not just trade it in? Selling your car at any price gives you the negotiating advantage of a straight, no-trade deal.

Set a time limit after which you will stop trying to sell your car. A decent time limit is 7 to 10 days; if the car does not sell by then it may be 6 months before it does. Don't forget, your car continues to depreciate all the while.

Exposure is important to sell anything. Once you set a price for your car, advertise it by every available means with the price right up front. Run short, punchy ads in your local paper emphasizing the car's most desireable features—low mileage, one owner, make and model, AM/FM radio—and include one descriptive adjective, such as *sacrifice, must sell,* or *bargain.* Place notices on bulletin boards at your office or local supermarkets. And, of course, place a *For Sale* sign in the window of the car itself. List your car with a professional referral service if one is available in your area. The fee for the service is usually based on a percentage of the final selling price. If there is a large flea market in your area, go as a customer, park your car with a *For Sale* sign on it near the activity, and browse around—let the car sell itself. Let all friends, neighbors, and relatives know you want to sell your car, and tell them to spread the word.

A phone number placed in a general public advertisement (such as in a newspaper) may swamp you with calls, but it does allow you to screen the callers before exposing your address to just anyone. This prevents unwanted visitors from appearing at your doorstep at any hour of the day or night. It further prevents your opening your front door to just anyone who may be posing as a buyer. Before you divulge your address to a potential buyer, get contact information on him: "Let me have your phone number and I'll call you right back."

If such precautions are not necessary, you may want to put your address in the ad and omit the phone number. Be specific about the times the car can be seen. This draws only the serious traffic to your home, and draws it when you want it.

An excellent source of prospects is the salesman who will be selling you your new car. If he can pick up an extra $20 by referring a customer to you, he will be more than happy for the opportunity. Even without a bird-dog fee, if he has a sale riding on whether or not you are able to sell your car, he will definitely have you in mind before he pitches someone out on the street unsold. (*Note:* Some states outlaw bird-dog fees.)

CONSUMMATING THE DEAL

If your customer has cash in his hand and you have the title in your hand, there are no complications; you simply trade what you have in your hand for what he has in his. But if you have a balance (such as a lien or encumbrance) with a lendor, and your buyer has a checkbook in hand, assurances are needed on both sides that you will pass clear title and that his check will not bounce. It is best to go to his bank together and have him cash a check (unless it is a loan assumption) or have him draw a certified check on his account made out in your name. Then go to your bank to pay off your loan, cancel the lien (or encumbrance) on your title, and transfer the title to his name. Procedures for transferring title, paying taxes, and obtaining fresh license plates for the car will vary from state to state. If a question comes up, call the AAA, a local new-car dealer, a justice of the peace, your court house, your attorney, a notary public, or a magistrate.

LET CHARLIE DO IT

Another way to sell your car is to put it on the lot of a "we will sell your car for you" dealer. The usual procedure is to pay a nominal registration fee when you place your car on the lot, and then pay a per diem charge until the car sells. When your car is sold by the dealer, you pay him either a flat fixed amount or a percentage of the price for which the car sold. Normally you decide at what price the car will finally be sold. You retain the right of refusal of any negotiating. You usually also retain the right to remove your car at any time with no loss to you other than the original registration fee and the per diem charges already paid.

To use this system successfully, you must get more for your car, after deductions for charges and fees, than you could have received for a trade allowance. The time factor is important; how long will it take to sell your car this way? This is a personal decision. Try it for 1 month, and if the car has not been sold, remove it from the lot and decide either to sell it yourself or to trade it in.

8
Handling the Salesman

THE SALESMAN

NEVER UNDERESTIMATE a salesman. In fact, the first thing you must realize—and appreciate—is just how well-trained most salesmen are. They have books, classes, sales meetings, videotapes, training seminars, and marketing and motivation institutes all designed for one purpose: to teach them how to separate you from your money. A salesman is taught to understand his customer and to make him want to buy, not tomorrow, but today.

In addition to book and classroom training, a salesman has day-to-day practical experience that gives him the opportunity to put his knowledge to use and practice on real people. There are also problem-solving clinics (usually sponsored and directed by the factory) in which salesmen from several dealerships get together and compare notes. Similar to group therapy, these discussions aim at solving mutual problems experienced by the participating salesmen regarding their handling of customers and closing of sales. Even though these salesmen are in direct competition with each other, they openly share their secrets and tactics, because the customer is the enemy.

How do you, the customer, stand a chance when you confront the salesman in a bargaining situation? Begin by approaching the entire situation with an open mind. Realize that everything the salesman does, you can do; his tactics and maneuvers become your tactics and maneuvers.

While working with a salesman, you should constantly ask yourself, "Am I being controlled and manipulated? Is the salesman interested only in my money? Do I really want what he is suggesting I take? Am I really going to receive what he says I am getting? Is he telling me a story or telling me the truth?'' Take the time and question: ''What is happening and why is it happening?''

SYSTEM SELLING

Salesmen are trained to use a system to sell a car: either a canned presentation or a selling cycle. A canned presentation is nothing more than a memorized speech someone else wrote. The salesman commits it to memory and mouths the words to the customer. An experienced salesman can give a canned sales talk and you would bet money he had never used those exact words on anyone else before. Your impression is that everything he says is spontaneous.

A salesman may subsidize a canned talk with a selling cycle or vice versa. A selling cycle is a step-by-step method of selling that allows the salesman to control his customer from start to finish. He will cover one area—one step of his system—and then move on to the next step. When the cycle is finished, it is extremely difficult to say no to his final request for the sale.

Salesmen who are fresh to the business are usually nervous about using a canned talk; they feel that you are aware that it is just that, a canned talk. The timing of a novice salesman is generally poor. He may start to say something entirely out of context to what is happening, stop himself in midsentence, and start off in another direction.

This could also happen to you as you read this book and acquire information and tactics foreign to your natural personality. You will then take them to a showroom and attempt to use them on a salesman. It is only normal for you to be a little nervous about doing so, and to miscue at times. However, like the salesman, with a little practice you will present your talk naturally and easily. It is important to be relaxed, to act as if you know exactly what you are saying, and to say it with confidence.

THE QUESTION PRINCIPLE

A salesman is trained to control his customer by asking questions. He is trained to answer questions by asking questions, and to seek a commitment to purchase by answering a question with a question that asks for the sale. If you are to control the salesman, you must learn to use the question principle.

When you ask, "Can I have the car tomorrow?" the salesman will probably answer you by asking, "Will you buy the car if I can have it ready for you by tomorrow?"

He has not really answered your question but rather set you up. Now you must either answer him or ask another question. If you simply say "yes" or "no," you have not received the answer to your question, but you have answered his question; you either buy or leave the door open to another question from the salesman. A suggested response is, "If I decided to buy the car, yes, I would want delivery within a day. Can you deliver the car within a day if we come to terms?" First, you get yourself off the hook; then you go back to your original question—as yet unanswered—and you have made no commitment.

He who asks the questions, controls the situation. When you ask a question that requires a lengthy response, it gives you a chance to think of your next question and it forces your adversary to stop and think. A question breaks up a salesman's pattern, interrupts his train of thought, and causes him to stop and give you an answer. As long as he is answering, he is not asking. This does not mean you should spend all your time asking questions for the sake of asking, nor does it mean that if a salesman asks you a question, you should refuse to answer him. How you react to a question asked by a salesman depends upon the type of question it is—whether it is a qualifying question or a commitment-seeking question.

There is a fine difference between qualifying you for need, want, and use of what you are looking for, and closing you on a particular car. Qualifying is simply finding out what you want, what is on your mind, and what it will take to make you happy; any good salesman should do this much. Closing is landing you on a particular car and asking purchase commitment questions.

Questions or statements like these are commitment seeking in nature:

"Will you . . . if I can . . . ?" Will you buy, if I can get the price reduced?

"Would you consider this?" Would you consider the blue car instead of the red?

"Would you like to?" Would you like to take it home today?

"Why don't you . . . ?" Why don't you give me a small deposit? Why don't you take it home today?

"Let's do this . . ." As if a group endeavor; watch this one, it's a fooler.

"Let me do this for you." Let me: write up your figures? take another $100 off the price? talk to my boss?

Questions like these are qualifying in nature:

"Do you want . . . ?"

"Have you seen. . . ?"

"What do you have now?"

"Who have you seen thus far?"

"Do you plan to do this?"

"What color, size, style?"

"Do you like this?"

Never hesitate to answer qualifying questions. A salesman must ask them if he is to give you the best he has to offer. If you are not ready to make a commitment, be evasive or simply do not answer commitment-seeking questions. The best way to avoid answering any question is to pretend that you did not hear it; change the subject or ask the salesman an irrelevant question. If the salesman asks too many personal questions, ask him whether you are there to buy a car or to file application for employment.

GAME PLAYING: WHY BOTHER?

It seems obvious that if you know what you want to buy, and what you are able to spend based on the computed cost of the car you want, all you need do is shop from dealer to dealer until you find the salesman willing to sell it to you at your price. Unfortunately, the salesmen you encounter will not know that you know and you cannot tell them that you know. If they are aware that you know, they will stubbornly hold out for a higher price: "This customer is not going to tell me how much profit I'm going to make."

Your task is to go along with the salesman and play the part that has been written for you. You must present the image of average Joe Public who has come in to be sold a car; not to buy, but to be sold. You must play the same games as the salesman, and you must, in the end, justify your position, just as the salesman must justify his offering to you.

There are certain moves that a salesman must make to successfully sell anyone a car. These inflexible moves give you a definite advantage, if for no other reason than that you can leave whenever you so desire; the salesman cannot. He must stay there and play the game.

A salesman will use the following procedure to try to sell a customer:

1. Approach. Butter up, warm up to, and relax the customer.
2. Qualify. Find out what the customer wants and needs.
3. Present and demonstrate. Touch it, see it, drive it.
4. Ask for the sale; write the order. "Will you buy from me today?"
5. Handle objections. Calm fears, close the sale, and ask for the sale.
6. Negotiate. "I will come down a little if you will come up a little."

7. Customer turnover. "I would like for you to meet my sales manager before you leave. Maybe he can give you the deal you want."

None of this means that since you know his next move you are to jump up and say, "I know what you are going to do next, aha! . . . . It means that you can plan your next several moves and that you can be better prepared to handle whatever he might toss in your direction. Whenever you see that you need time to coordinate a counterattack, ask a question that requires a lengthy answer.

JUDGING THE SALESMAN

There is such a thing as gut instinct, which tells you on first meeting whether or not you like someone. There is usually a reason why you may have a first and immediate bad impression of a salesman before a full sentence is spoken. It may be subconscious feedback: the salesman reminds you of someone with whom you once had a bad experience or, for whatever reason, did not like. These are feelings that must be recognized and set aside. Let the salesman prove himself to you before you pass judgment.

The two most important assets of a good salesman are the ability to communicate and product knowledge. If the salesman does not know what he is selling, he is no good to you. Likewise, he is no good if he knows what he is selling but cannot convey that message to you.

A salesman should sell in a relaxed manner, for his job is to make your purchase comfortable, not tense. If the salesman is making you feel uneasy, is not alleviating your fears, and is not relaxing you, he is not doing his job well at all. And it all begins with the approach.

A salesman is taught to be friendly, courteous, and prompt in his approach to you when you walk onto the showroom floor. The two of you are total strangers, so the salesman must become "old friends" with you as quickly as possible. The first few minutes are critical. This is when you decide whether or not you like the salesman and can trust him, and whether or not you want to put your money in his pocket.

While you are deciding about him, he is deciding about you. It is imperative that you realize it is to your advantage to make a favorable impression on the salesman. It will make a definite difference in the deal you are offered when you sit down to negotiate.

Your approach to a salesman should be enthusiastic and friendly. Never be withdrawn, bashful, reticent, or hesitant. The enthusiasm you display can ruin a salesman's timing and throw his procedure completely off track. He will hesitate to do anything which might turn your enthusiasm off. If you want to buy out of procedure and rearrange the normal order of presentation, that is all right with the salesman, provided you continue to display an interest in buying his product. Quite frankly, you can do almost anything you want to do as long as you act as if you are going to buy.

The salesman must find out, as quickly as he can, where you are from, where you were born, where you work, whether you are single or married, and how many children you have. Why is it so important and how does he go about it?

A salesman will usually begin by casually asking, "Are you from this area?" You reply, "No, I am from Hometown." And the dialogue continues, "Oh, were you born there?" "No, I was born in Nextown," you answer. "Where do you work?" "I work for Big Corp, Inc. I am an engineer." "Have you worked for Big Corp very long?" "Well, going on 11 years now, if you consider that a long time." "Are you married?" "Yes, I am." "Do you have any children?" "Yes, we have three." And so on—question after question. A salesman will not machine-gun the questions as above but will space them out and make appropriate comment as he goes along. And all the questions and answers do mean something.

The Serious Customer. Salesmen are trained to be extremely observant. Within the first few minutes after you meet, the salesman looks for indicators that you are a serious buyer worthy of his time. The more positive indicators he finds, the more time he will spend helping you. This is important, for if he does not believe you are serious, he will try to land you on the first car he presents and get you to sit down and sign up, which you will interpret as pushiness.

If you want a salesman to think you are a serious buyer and treat you as such, it will do no harm to set up a few props, a few visible indications that you are a right-now buyer. An older car, worn-out tires, a close-to-expiration safety lane sticker, a cleaned-out trunk or glove box, snow tires not on by November (in northern states), a rough idle, an almost empty fuel tank, a checkbook or title in your shirt pocket—all indicate "ready to buy today."

The Nonserious Customer. If there are indicators that show you to be a serious buyer, there must be indicators that show you as nonserious—just a looker. A classic example is the married person who walks onto a showroom floor alone. If you are married, a salesman may find out by spotting a wedding ring or may acquire a clue from your trade-in: an infant seat, children's clothes, or toys in the back seat. A salesman may ask forthrightly, "Are you married?" You respond that you are. He will then determine whether you have a valid reason for being there alone: "Is your spouse working right now?" You reply, "No, he/she is home with the children." If he/she were working, the salesman would classify you as a serious buyer, for you have a legitimate reason for being there alone. However, if your spouse is home with the kids, you are probably a nonserious customer. If you were a serious buyer you would have your spouse with you.

Another indicator that you are not serious is the little notebook that pops out of your pocket every 5 minutes on which you make notes about price, options, and so on. This is a strong indicator that you are merely shopping. It tells the salesman that you are only compiling information right now and that if he lets you leave he has only a slim chance of ever seeing you again. You may receive a low-ball figure to ensure your return.

Your best move is to bring the notebook to the salesman's attention yourself, rather than have him catch you trying to sneak a few figures down when his back is turned. As you bring the book out for the first time, show it to the salesman (the notebook, not the contents), and say, "I'm going to take a few notes as we go along so that when we sit down for the final paperwork I won't forget anything we have covered." This tells him the notebook is for his benefit as well as your own.

Knowing where you are from gives the salesman an idea of your affluence (or lack of it), social standing, and cultural background. Everything tells the salesman something; if you drive up in a 10-year-old car and live on the wrong side of the tracks, the salesman will quickly determine your degree of sincerity and ability to buy before he wastes his time and effort showing, demonstrating, and trying to sell you a new car. These are all signs that help the salesman decide what he will or will not do for you, what he will or will not show you, and whether or not he will give you a demonstration ride. The more he knows about you, the more he can help you, and the more productive his selling will be. And time is money.

Common Opening Statements. Do not say "I am just looking," or "I am just shopping." Both indicate that you are a nonserious buyer just wasting the salesman's time. His first thought is that you have nothing better to do so you are killing time looking at new cars, or that your only interest is to get another price to add to your long list. Both give him little hope for a sale, and little motivation to be cooperative. Open with, "I am interested in seeing one of your (whatever it is)."

Never say, "I am paying straight cash. This tells the salesman he will not have to worry about the finance profit the dealership makes, which is about 20 percent of the total finance charge. A salesman/dealer will give away more gross profit if he knows from the start he will be making the finance profit. Lead the salesman to believe he will make the finance profit by immediately asking, "Can we finance our purchase here or will we have to go to a bank?"

THE DIRECT APPROACH

There is an approach known as the direct approach that, when used properly, saves everybody a lot of time and effort and eliminates a lot of wear and tear on the nervous system. The direct approach can be used only on a straight, no-trade purchase. It is literally impossible to lay it on the line if a trade is involved, for it is too easy for a salesman to juggle and switch figures around. Never attempt to use the direct approach on a factory-order purchase.

Here's what to do: Walk onto the showroom floor, make a general approach or introduction to the salesman, and tell him, "You have a sale if you will take a $200 gross profit deal. Will you take a two-buck deal?" And then shut up.

The ball is in his lap and he must now say yes, no, or maybe. If he says maybe, continue with, "I know exactly what I want, and I have no trade-in, no tricks, no games. If you will take my deal, fine. If you will not, then say so and I will find someone who will. I'll figure my own deal and I'll compensate for your floor plan charge if necessary. I'll finance it through your dealership, so you will make the finance profit also. Fair enough? Will you do it?"

If he says no, you have the option to leave or try back-up Plan A. Plan A is to find out what kind of deal the salesman will take. "If you will not take a $200 deal, how close will you come?" If the salesman still balks, still does not seem to want to play, then leave. If he does give you a gross profit figure, decide at that time whether it is close enough to satisfy you. You might get lucky and select a car that has just come off the truck, so you will not have to pay a floor plan charge and can afford to give a little on the gross.

If he says yes, he will take a $200 quickie, tell him to check with his sales manager right now, to be sure he will be able to obtain approval on a $200 deal if you write one. Ninety-nine percent of the time a salesman will not be authorized to give a low gross deal to a customer without management approval. You must make it perfectly clear, from the start, that you mean business and that you expect him to also. Then let him show you his stock.

From the nature of your approach, the salesman and his sales manager must assume that you are a sharp trader. They may, however, take the chance that you are bluffing and try to sell you their car at their price. They may go along with you, start to finish, until you prove that you do know what you are doing. At that point they may put pressure on you to see it their way, or flatly refuse to give you the deal, or sigh in resignation and give you the deal exactly as you write it. Their final effort will be something like this: "Look, we simply cannot give you the deal you want; we can give you a $300 deal." From there they will work their way down, $10 at a time, until you finally yield and say, "Okay, I'll take it." For the extra effort made to wear you down, they could make an extra $50. For the sake of a little patience on your part, you can save the fifty and get the deal you want.

Salesmen are cautious of the quickie sale, especially if the person walks in and starts talking buy, buy, buy before he has looked, touched, and driven. The person who tries to move this fast usually does his thinking after the fact. It can therefore be difficult for you to use this direct approach on a salesman, for he will not initially read you as a serious, educated buyer. He will read you as a quickie customer who plans to bluff his way through the sale. You must convince him you are indeed serious, that you are knowledgeable, and that you know what you are doing. How much convincing you must do depends on the individual salesman with whom you are dealing.

THE IMPLIED APPROACH

The most effective approach, with or without a trade-in, is the subtle, implied approach. You lay nothing on the line, make no commitments, and give no ultimatum, yet you set the stage to write the deal you want.

To lay it on the line is to say, "Look, I know you can take $400 off the sticker price. How much better can you do?"

To make a commitment is to say, "If you take $400 off the sticker price, I will buy the car today."

To give an ultimatum is to say, "If you cannot take $400 off the sticker, I do not want to do business with you; I will leave. How about it?"

Any of these approaches will receive a response, but not necessarily the response you expect. To lay it on the line makes the salesman defensive and argumentative. He will say to himself and then to you, "Why should

I take any more off the sticker, even if I want to take the $400 off?'' The salesman may then decide that he will give no higher a discount than he absolutely must.

To make a commitment or give an ultimatum kills any chance for negotiating. If the salesman says, ''Okay, I can take $400 off the sticker; do you want the car right now or do you want to pick it up in an hour?'' you just bought a car. You cannot say, ''I just wanted to see if you would take that much off the price.'' The salesman will physically throw you off the lot.

To use the implied approach is to say, ''Are you running a special promotion this week or are you just giving your normal discounts?'' (Smile when you ask.) You automatically imply that, promotion or not, the salesman always discounts his merchandise and that it is a fixed (normal) amount. Now, no matter what he says, he loses negotiating strength. If he says, ''We do not discount,'' he will lose you completely; you will go to a dealer who does discount. If he says, ''No promotions, just our usual discounts,'' you may now come back with, ''And what is your company policy regarding discounts?'' Or, ''What are your normal discounts?'' and go from there.

Implied approach is implied consent. Any answer to an implied consent question benefits the person asking. Regardless of the answer given, it implies consent, acceptance, and agreement. Implied consent always consists of a choice of two options. ''Do you want to take the car home tonight or pick it up tomorrow?'' Whichever answer you give, you just bought a car. The salesman implies that you have made the decision to buy, that there is no question about it, and that he just wants to clarify the details of delivery.

Since you will be using implied consent, you must always assume that the answer you want is already there, and that all you are doing is clarifying the details. This principle is particularly effective in the service department, but it can be used anywhere throughout your purchase activities, from approach through negotiations. ''Are you going to give me floor mats for the front and back or just for the front?'' ''Are you going to give me another $100 off or a free rustproofing?'' (On a used car: ''Are you going to tune up the engine or change the oil?'') Use your imagination on this one; it is wide open.

COMMUNICATING

The act of communicating and establishing an understanding is important, both for the customer and for the salesman. Communication that secures an understanding between the two of you will be easier and each of you will feel more comfortable if you seem to be of the same caliber of intelligence. Always attempt to talk on the same level as the salesman, but to a point. If the salesman uses gutter language, you may not want to come down to his level. If, however, he uses simple terms to express himself, then adjust to his level. Always maintain good eye contact with the salesman when communicating. Poor eye contact indicates introversion, or the fact that you have something to hide. Do not look down or to the side when you speak, or walk away trailing a sentence. Be brief, keep points simple, speak clearly and distinctly, and think before you open your mouth.

It is imperative that you have a few select phrases to toss at a salesman to firm up what he is trying to tell you and, when necessary, to bring the conversation down to earth; salesmen are well known for small talk, evasiveness, and double talk. When a salesman says, "You know what I mean?" or, "You do understand, don't you?" simply reply, "No, I do not know what you mean. Could you be a little more specific? Could you explain that in greater detail? Would you mind telling me exactly what you mean by that? What are you trying to tell me?" This will tell the salesman to quit playing games. It also lets him know that you want the whole story, not just part of it, and that he can be specific without being lengthy. If you do not understand something, question it. His intention may be to confuse you by talking around the issue. By remaining silent rather than admitting ignorance of what he is saying, you let the salesman be successful in his effort to sidestep the matter.

STRATEGIES AND PRECAUTIONS

Placing the salesman on the defensive makes him apologetic, makes him explain, makes him give promises, and makes him defend his position—all to your advantage. The more he says, the more he must live up to, not only while you are negotiating the deal, but after the sale as well. It also uncovers hidden information that a salesman would otherwise not offer. Where there is defense there is offense. While the salesman is defending, you are definitely on the offense. As long as he is defending, he is talking, which gives you time to plan your next move and think of your next question, and time to analyze what is happening. It slows the salesman down and interrupts his selling cycle. The technique is simple enough if you follow a few basic rules. First, a question of general interest relative to after-the-purchase service.

"How is your service department?" you ask.

"Our service department is tops in the area," he replies. (Statement)

"People have told me that your service department is not too good, that they have had a few problems and are not all that happy." (Statement, set up).

"Oh no, I cannot imagine who could say that or why they would say it." (Defense) "All my customers are well taken care of when they need service. I personally see to it." (Implied promise)

"Then what you are saying is that if I buy a car from you, I can expect excellent service, and you will personally see to it. Is that right?" (Confirmation)

"Part of getting good service depends upon how well a salesman gets along with the service manager and the service personnel. I get along well with all of them, so you need not worry about the service you are going to get." (Direct promise)

A salesman has been trained to handle problem areas quickly and then to get off the subject or sidestep the issue. If you do not receive the answers, (the promises you desire), you may find it necessary to reopen the issue, so ask again:

"Well, if there is one thing that means a lot to me, it is good service. I don't want to have to argue with a service manager each time I need something done to my car. Can you assure me that I will get good service?"

"Look, buy the car from me and I promise you good service. Is that fair enough?" (Firm promise)

Now the salesman has no choice but to back up his promise. If he does not, you have every right to hold him personally responsible for any bad service you might receive during warranty coverage. A salesman knows whether his service department is good, mediocre, or bad. If it is bad, he will hesitate to make a firm commitment that you will receive good service.

You may prefer third-party evidence to get the answer you need: "People have told me that your service department is not very good." If the salesman says, "Yes, I know our service is not the best in the country, but what can I do about it?" you have the answer you need. If he is evasive and says, "Our service is no worse than that of any other service department in the area," again, you have the answer you need, because he is implying that his service department is not quite up to snuff. If he quickly and strongly defends his service by stating, "It is the best in the area—second to none," chances are that it is.

A statement such as, "I hear you are having trouble with this particular model" brings about interesting conversation. If there are major problems with the model and the salesman knows about them, he will go right along with you and agree; he may even tip you off to exactly what the problems are. If there are no problems that he knows of, he may question you about exactly what problems you have heard about. In that instance, you need only plead ignorant to the facts to get off the hook. "I don't know exactly what the problems are; some friends of mine told me this model is not a very great car," or "They told me that you were having a few problems with this model—a few bugs not yet worked out." That is a relatively safe statement, for every car has at least one bug.

Any statement or question that begins with, "I have heard," "I understand this or that," "Is it true that," or "Is this the model that" requires a response and defense. This weakens a salesman's negotiating strength, for no matter what he does he will never be completely certain how important any fear or objection you express is to you. In the closing room, while he plans what deal to present, he will be thinking of all the negatives you have presented.

When you need honest, sincere advice from a salesman, you do not always know that it will be the best he has to offer, and that it is, in fact, honest. A simple, "Help me make up my mind," is too vague and too open to make a salesman stop and think before he gives you advice.

In this instance, you must play a little dumb ("I do not know that much about cars"), appeal to the salesmam's ego ("I would appreciate it if you would give me your thoughts on this matter"), use a little flattery ("You are in the business, and you should know exactly which car is best for me"), put him on the spot and force him to give you honest advice ("Could you give me your honest opinion on this"), reward him for doing a good job ("I will really appreciate it and it will mean a sale for you"), punish him for a bad job ("Of course if you give me bad advice, I will not be happy, and I will tell you how unhappy I am every day that your doors are open. You will have to listen to me knowing all the time that I will not be buying my next car from you"), and participate and work together toward a common goal ("Do you think we can put our heads together and see what you think will be our best course of action," or "Let's sit down and see what we can come up with").

Be wary of the good-is-good and bad-is-good salesman. As far as he is concerned, whether you like it and want it or do not like it and do not want it, you are smart for your decision. If you comment favorably about disc brakes, the salesman will tell you how wise you are for wanting disc brakes. That same salesman will tell you how wise you are for liking drum-type brakes if you say you do not like disc brakes. Advice from this type of person might as well not have been given, for it is offered only to encourage your purchase and to help you justify what you are doing. Treat the advice lightly, and do not let it influence your final decisions. It will help if you tell the salesman that no one item will destroy your plans to buy his car, and that you are really looking for serious, constructive advice. As always, it is best to solicit multiple opinions rather than one opinion given for the sake of profit.

PAY PLANS

A salesman is paid when you buy a car from him, but he does not necessarily clean up on every sale he makes. Much depends upon how much was made on the deal (gross profit for the dealer) or how many units the salesman sells within a month (sometimes based on weekly production). It is important to be aware of how a salesman is paid, since it can have a definite effect upon the deal you are offered.

There are two major pay plans for car salesmen: the percent-of-gross plan and the per-unit-sold plan.

Under the percent-of-gross plan, the salesman receives a fixed percentage (usually 25 percent) computed against the actual gross profit made on each car he sells. The more profit he makes on the deal, the fatter his paycheck will be. A $400 gross profit deal gives him $100.

Under the per-unit-sold plan, the salesman receives a fixed number of dollars per car sold, regardless of the gross profit made. This amount will vary between dealers and is usually tied to a bonus system to reward high-volume sales production.

Before you can use this information, you must find out how your particular salesman is paid. Needless to say, you cannot bluntly ask, "How are you paid?" You must make the salesman think you are merely interested in the automobile industry in general. Lead into your real question by telling a story or asking a series of small questions. "You know, Mr. Salesman, I thought of being a car salesman at one time. It seems like it could be very lucrative. You work on a commission basis, don't you?" He will answer yes, and you continue, "I am just curious, but how is your commission determined? Do you get so much for each car you sell? Does it make any difference whether I buy a cheap car or an expensive car?" Or, "My brother-in-law told me that car salesmen are paid only when they sell and that they get only a small percentage of the profit. Is that true?" Either approach should yield the information you want.

When you have the information you want, file it for future reference. What you must remember is that the salesman who works on percent of gross will try to get every dollar out of the deal that he can. His income is directly geared to gross profit made. Every dollar he adds to the basic deal is 25¢ in his pocket. Twenty-five cents sounds menial, but a $200 negotiated difference on a deal will put an extra $50 right into his pocket when he convinces you to accept his deal. The credibility of the percent-of-gross salesman is to be questioned at all times, regardless of his sincerity. When he tells you that he is going to try to force his sales manager to accept your terms, can you really believe him? Conversely, the salesman who is paid per unit sold could hardly care less for what price any given car sells. When this salesman tells you that he will do everything he can to get you the deal you want, he usually means it. The per-unit-sold salesman will also be more inclined to make a sincere effort to get you the extras you would like tacked onto the deal as freebies; he will be more inclined to tell his sales manager that the sale hinges upon whether or not you get the freebie. He does not care if his sales manager must give something away to make the sale as long as it does not affect his car count for the month.

BYPASS THE SALESMAN?

Some people think they will get a better deal if they bypass the salesman and deal direct with upper management. They feel that if the dealership does not have to pay a salesman a commission, the savings will be passed on to them. In other words, eliminate the middleman and automatically save money. Quite the contrary. You will pay more when you deal with management than if you deal and negotiate with a salesman.

Most dealerships turn all deals over to the salesman who was "up" on the floor when the deal was written and signed, so if the salesman is going to be paid on these house accounts (deals written by management) anyway there is no savings to be passed on. Even if a dealership retains house accounts and does not pay the salesman, you will still save no money, for the house is going to make as much as possible on each and every deal that is written.

Normal dealership procedure is to turn you over to a salesman with a brief introduction stating who you are and what you plan to buy. This is the same salesman with whom you would have nothing to do a few minutes earlier—the one you chose to ignore. What a small world. What kind of job do you think he is going to do for you? He knows what you tried to do and he knows that you couldn't care less about him. You could consider an appeal for mercy.

By going directly to management you lose negotiating strength, since you can hardly stand there and argue with a manager in the same manner you can argue price, trade allowance, and terms with a salesman. You have approached management because you trust them (friend to friend), and, because you know them and they know you, you trust them to write a fair deal for you. This intrinsic trust gives management an edge in the matter, plus extra profit. You do not question the deal that is offered to you and you assume that the figures quoted are nonnegotiable. If you have bypassed the salesman you cannot use him as a runner and a go-between to management for your negotiations. It is infinitely easier to walk away from a salesman than it is to walk away from that friend you have in management when you decide to "think about it."

The best course of action is to get yourself off the hook from the beginning. Approach the salesman and tell him that you know someone in management, but that you don't want him to lose his commission on your purchase. The salesman will know his dealership's policy regarding house accounts and will either work you or immediately turn you over to management. If he works you and management later chooses not to credit him with the sale, that is a conflict between the salesman and the dealership; you incur no blame for the lost commission. Because you expressed concern for him, the salesman will bend over backward to help you before, during, and after the sale. Keep him on your side.

APATHETIC SALESMEN

Apathetic salesmen are salesmen with an aloof attitude who act as if they are doing you a favor by selling you a car. They are cold and unresponsive to you and your needs. When, by chance, you encounter this type of salesman, you will not want to stay, let alone do business with him. There are several ways to handle the bad salesman.

1. Leave the showroom immediately and shop another dealership.
2. Ask to speak to his sales manager. When you meet him, tell him that you are not happy with the salesman and request that another salesman handle you.
3. Leave, and return when the salesman you do not like is not on duty. When all is said and done, advise management of your experience with the first salesman and how close they came to losing your business.

9
Negotiating

BEFORE YOU WHEEL AND DEAL

NEGOTIATING BEGINS WITH your first contact with the salesman. He is beginning to set you up for the close (asking for sale and signature) as early as the initial handshake. Your concern and effort is to set him up, and this begins with the demonstration ride and product inspection. (See page 91 for additional information.)

Even though you are looking at new cars, do not assume that they all drive, handle, and feel alike. Drive at least three of the same model and equipment—all with power steering or without; all with the same size engine and type of transmission. Subject them all to the same roads and conditions. You will notice a slight difference in the handling and feel among the three, but you will get a good idea of how the basic model should perform. One may stand out as the worst of the three and naturally you would reject it.

Driving three or more of the same model also lets you develop a list of objections (small annoyances) that will strengthen your negotiations. There has to be at least one thing wrong with each car—a squeak or a rattle; a steering pull to one side; uncomfortable seats; radio static; a clutch that is spongy or soft or hard; an engine that stalls, hesitates, has a rough idle, or is nonresponsive; or something that is too tight or too loose.

Make comments as you drive, such as: "Do they all pull to one side like this? Do they all idle this rough? I don't like the way this corners. This clutch feels funny. Do they all shift this slowly?" Back on the lot you can continue: "The trunk is too small; the head room and leg room are not quite good enough." And don't forget the standard equipment:

66

"I don't like power brakes, and that's the only way this comes, isn't it? I could do without a vinyl roof. I just can't see paying for something I don't really need. But I do like the car, sort of. Well, if the price is good enough, I guess I can live with it."

When you finally decide on the car you want, meticulously check it out bumper to bumper, and drive it twice—before you negotiate and before you sign anything. Even if the dealer is making half what he would normally make on a new-car deal, you still have the right to demand a blemish-free car. The factory picks up the tab on blemishes anyway. Any flaws you find enhance your negotiating strength. Remember:

1. Check all equipment on the car against the factory label (sticker), to be sure everything is on the car at the time you sign to buy it.

2. Itemize all optional equipment in your notebook and transfer the list onto your purchase contract, including the serial number of the car you are buying. A switch is possible without the serial number.

3. Be prepared to take the car home the same day you buy it. If you leave it overnight, you may find equipment has been switched by the time you take delivery. Steel-belted tires become glass-belted tires; an AM/FM becomes an AM radio.

4. Disregard any extras that are not on the factory label, such as dealer handling charges, equipment additions, road test charges, rustproofing or undercoat, and any switches of equipment that may have been made.

CLOSING THE SALE

The Closing Room. This is where the salesman does his real selling, where you do your real bargaining, where approvals are made and signatures ink the paper, and money changes hands. This is where all hard-core negotiating takes place, where the final deal is given birth. All that preceded was only in preparation for the closing room.

Never fear the closing room. If the salesman is to make the sale that lets you own the car you want, you must sit down together and negotiate, talk it over, work things out. Here are a few common closing approaches and appeals used by salesmen. They are basically simple in design, but the effect and impact they have on your negotiations is not.

1. The sympathy close. There are three types of sympathy close. One is an appeal to your sympathetic nature by the salesman. "Feel sorry for me and buy; sales are down; I have not been making enough money to support my family; I have a wife and three children who

are hungry,'' and on and on. The salesman who uses the emotionally charged sympathy close does not deserve the sale.

The second-sympathy close involves a factory- or company-sponsored contest or bonus the salesman will receive if he gets just one more sale. Sometimes the contest or bonus is real and sometimes it is not. The key to this close is for the salesman to create a sense of urgency where none exists; you might as well buy the car now and help the salesman win the contest or receive the bonus. This close plays upon your sympathetic nature to "help the salesman out" and is used by salesmen who spot a person with a charitable personality. Do what is convenient for you. If you are not inclined to buy on that very day, tell the salesman he will have to find someone else to help him win his contest or bonus.

The third sympathy close uses reverse sympathy; the salesman wants to make you feel sorry for yourself and to convince you that the only way to ease your sorrow is to buy his product. He may approach this close in a variety of ways but the most frequently used is the "you owe it to yourself" approach.

Just consider what it is that you owe yourself. Do you owe yourself a monthly payment that will burden your budget? Do you owe yourself a car that is not really what you want and need? Think before you leap. Self-indulgence is all right, provided it does not bury you.

2. My boss. A frequently used close is this: "I am mad at my boss today. I do not care if the company makes money on this deal or not. I am going to see that you get the highest discount anyone can get." Just like that. The salesman is mad at his boss, and even though his paycheck depends upon how much he makes on the deal (gross profit), he is going to do special favors for you, a stranger.

Now, unfortunately for you, the price he just quoted is the best that he can obtain; if he could do better, he surely would because he is mad at his boss.

He may turn it around: "My boss is in a good mood today, so we will have no trouble getting the trade allowance you want. Now, the book says that your car is worth $3,000, but I am going to do everything I can to get you the $3,300 you want" (setup). Good mood or bad, his sales manager looks at the numbers with detached emotion. Profit is profit, and he will write as much as he thinks he can get. When the salesman returns, he will begin with, "Well, he is in a better mood than I thought. As I told you, the book value on

your car is $3,000. I was able to talk him into giving you an allowance of $3,110'' (look at the difference: $190 less than you want).
3. Oh, brother. The salesman may use the "brother" approach. "Can I talk to you like a brother? If you were my brother, I would give you this advice." Or, "I am going to treat you like my own brother. I will give you the same deal I would give my own brother."

The "brother" approach is designed to eliminate doubt and close the credibility gap between you and the salesman. When you doubt his sincerity, you need assurances that he is doing nothing different from what he would do with any other customer. Pass over this story as if the salesman had said nothing. His sales manager does not care if he is dealing with a brother, sister, in-law, or whomever; he looks only at profit—"How much are we going to make on this deal?"
4. The green bean. "I am new in this business." Veteran salesmen use this ploy to lower the guard of either a hostile customer or a very quiet customer. If you know you are dealing with a 15-year veteran salesman, you will resist his closing attempts, and you will fear being sold or pressured into making a decision. Conversely, you will feel relaxed and confident around a novice. In the back of your mind your pride and ego whispers, "I can handle this guy." You are therefore relaxed and are not prepared to do battle with an experienced veteran salesman. Be wary of an admission of being new to the business, for most green salesmen will not admit this. They usually want to give the impression of experience.
5. The other customer. To create urgency to buy, a salesman may invent another person who is interested in the car you want. The other person will either be his sales manager or another salesman. The phone will ring and the scenario begins: "Yes, Mr. Jones, I still have that car in stock. In fact, I have a customer sitting here right now who is thinking of buying it. (Pause) No, he hasn't bought it yet. (Pause) Well, how soon can you get here? (Pause) No, I cannot put a hold on the car for you. It is first come, first served. If this gentleman decides to buy it you will just have to buy another one. (Pause) Well, let me check with my sales manager and see what he has to say about holding it for you. But it is really first come, first served."

Obviously you do not want to lose the car and your first impulse will be to tell the salesman to tell the other customer that you just bought it. Don't do it. Consider that there are other cars on his lot equally as nice. If there is another customer interested in that particular car, let him have it. If the salesman truly had someone else interested, he would not make it first come, first served; he would make it, "Which deal will give me the highest profit?"

Tell the salesman to go ahead and let the other guy have the car. When he hangs up tell him that you are going to sit there until the guy shows up, and that you will not buy anything else until you are sure that car is sold. How long you sit and wait is entirely up to you. Or you can stand up and walk away as if to leave the dealership. When the salesman asks where you are going, simply tell him you are going to another dealer to buy a car at your price.

6. Today only. In a closing or negotiating situation, the salesman may tell you that his sales manager will give you the car you want, the way you want it, for a certain price, but "Only if you buy today. If you come back tomorrow you will not get the same deal." Your first instinct is to say, "If he will sell it to me today for that price, he will sell it to me tomorrow for the same price." To which the salesman will reply, "Look, I've seen him do this before and the customer did not believe he meant it. The next day when he returned, my sales manager refused to give him the car for the same price he had quoted the day before. My sales manager wants your business today, not tomorrow, and he is willing to bend a little to get it. Let's face it; he knows that you may not come back if you leave now. So how about it; let's send you home in your new car today." (Confirmation, appeal to logic, commitment seeking, implied consent.)

It sounds fairly convincing; however, if you leave and return the next day you will be able to get the car at the quoted, lower, today-only price. If the sales manager can sell the car today for a profit, he will not turn that same profit away 24 hours later. To let you walk away is to let you cool off, shop around, change your mind, or ask for a better deal. So he must do everything he can to sign you up today.

7. The sound of silence. When a good salesman asks a closing question (asks for the sale), he will shut up and wait for your answer. If he is a second-class salesman he will ask a closing question and then, before you can answer, butt in with further comment. The logic of silence is that whoever speaks first, loses the battle. If you say yes, he has a sale. If you say no, he will ask, "Why not" which eventually leads to another closing question. If you say nothing, he will sit in silence until you do speak. Your options are:

1. Say yes, no, or maybe.
2. Say anything else—change the subject.
3. Say nothing at all—the sound of silence.
4. Answer his question with a question.

Saying, yes, no, or maybe gives the salesman reentry to the situation and another chance to close you. Saying nothing at all creates enormous tension. The salesman has absolutely no idea what you are thinking, whether you were ready for a closing question or not, or whether or not he has just blown the sale. He thinks you are spending this silent time thinking of *not* buying, and planning how you are going to tell him. The longer the silence, the more he will believe just that. Sooner or later, someone must say something. If you clam up completely you may get a slightly better deal, if it is possible for the salesman to give you one. Changing the subject offers temporary relief and relieves the salesman of the effort of trying to close you for a while. He must handle your subject change and then work himself around to another closing question. Answering his question with a question opens doors for further discussion. The question you ask need not be remotely related to the question he just asked. In fact, if it is unrelated, it directs the course of the conversation away from a close and puts you in control. Strategically, the more questions you ask, the less selling the salesman can do.

8. An answer to every objection. Do not think for a moment that you are unique in having reasons for not buying, or in knowing ways to attempt to get away from a salesman. A good salesman has heard them all. And he has an answer to every one of them. The following excuses and stalls show what is commonly used and how the salesman will react.

"We want to think about it. We want to talk it over—we will let you know tomorrow." The salesman's response: "Exactly what do you want to think about? What do you want to talk over? If you need to talk it over, you can do that much right here. I'll leave you two alone and you call me when you are ready."

"I have to go home and talk it over with my wife—I will let you know tomorrow." The salesman's response: "What exactly do you want to talk over? Can't you make the decision without her? Here is a phone; call her right now and talk it over. Is she home right now? Let's take the car to your house and show it to her; it will give you a chance to drive it again."

"The price is too high." The salesman presumes that you do not know how much is too much, so he will ask two questions: "Is it too high because you cannot afford to spend that much?" Or, "Is it too high because you can get a better price from another dealer?" If the price is more than you can afford, he will try to switch you to a less expensive model. If another dealer can give you a better deal, he will attempt to beat the other dealer with amenities—you should pay more to get better service, better salesman, better dealership, and so on.

All excuses are rebutted in a manner that puts the salesman in control. He will ferret out the real reason why you want to leave without buying and force you to give another reason "why not" until you run out of reasons.

When you want to leave, you will find the "sleep on it" excuse very effective. Tell the salesman that you never buy anything without sleeping on it. He can hardly offer to let you sleep at his dealership overnight to reach your final decision.

If you are with someone—spouse, fiancée, or friend—and need to get off the hook, simply start an argument with whomever is with you. This can be fun if you can put on a good act. Few salesmen will dare butt into an argument of this nature. Begin with a simple disagreement: You like blue and she likes red. Then get into the heavy stuff—the major differences of opinion.

If a salesman is persistent, you may have to tell him bluntly, "I do not like pushy salesmen, and I would never buy from a pushy salesman. If you want me to buy your product, we will work at my speed, and my speed is not ready to buy today."

WHEELING AND DEALING

Negotiating. Negotiating is trying to save a few bucks on a purchase that you are going to make anyway. The decision to buy has generally been made when you sit down to work out the price and terms of the purchase. It may, at times, be a conditional decision ("If the price is right, I will buy"), but it is, nevertheless, a decision. Once you have made a decision to buy, your negotiations may be weakened by the fact that you want the car, and that it is difficult to separate the decision to buy from the decision to buy at a specific price. If you want the car badly enough, you will pay almost any price for it; you will not hold out for a $50- better deal if you are led to believe you will lose the car for holding out.

If the dealer is trying to make a killing on the deal, you must consider the fact that there are other cars at other dealers and mentally be prepared to continue to look and shop until you find the price that satisfies you.

Do's & Don'ts. When you decide to go ahead and buy your next new car, wash your old car, mow your lawn, clean out your garage, straighten your house or apartment, and take a cool bath or shower. These actions will help you to carry over the success attitude when you sit down with a salesman to work a deal. As you clear the clutter around you, the mind automatically becomes less cluttered and functions more properly. Things seem to go your way and you pursue what you want with more confidence.

Psychologically, you will negotiate with more confidence if you have the cash in your pocket (a bank account will do as well) when you are firming up a deal. You will have more self-confidence, for you are spending real, cash-out-of-pocket money, not just numbers on paper. You will be more cautious about throwing your money away on an impulse purchase. If you have the money in hand, your attitude toward the salesman will become, "I have the money and you must be very nice to me if you want it. You will have to give me a super deal before I turn my cash over to you." (However, do not tell the salesman you have cash. He must think you plan to give him the finance profit.)

When negotiating, you must always be talking about a specific car. Do not choose a car at random just to have a car with which to test the salesman's figures. Pick the car you would buy provided the salesman and you get together on the terms. His discount, trade allowance, and terms quoted mean nothing if they are for a car that you do not care to buy, and they cannot be used to accurately compare one dealer against another.

Never ask for anything and expect to receive it after you have signed on the dotted line. If the salesman includes something, at your request, after you have signed, it is for appearance's sake alone. His immediate response to you will be, "I will put it right here and do the best I can to get it for you." His first words to his sales manager will be, "He asked for it after he signed the contract, so we can scratch that off right now." When you signed, you bought, and anything after that is forgotten by the salesman and his sales manager.

Never ask a salesman to "try" to do anything for you. Always make it seem as if the entire deal hinges upon his ability to perform; if he does not produce results, you will not buy. "Try to get this for me" tells the salesman that you will buy whether you get it or not. When he returns with the deal, he will tell you he "tried," which is all you asked. "Do you think" is just as bad. "Do you think your sales manager will give me extra (whatever)?" This is telling the salesman, "I do not think he will; do you?" The salesman will say, "I do not think he will, but I will try my best to get it for you. Now, just sign here and I'll see what I can do."

If you want a freebie added to the deal, by all means ask for it, but keep it short and to the point. "Mr. Salesman, your figures are good, the price is right, the trade allowance is what I had in mind. Now, I will buy the car today if you will include (whatever) as part of the deal." Not "throw in" and not "give me," but "include as part of." This throws the ball in his lap, and he must make a response. If he says no, or if he tries to talk you out of the freebie, he may lose the deal. Your job is to make him believe that you will not buy without the freebie.

Never use, "I cannot afford it," to get an extra $50 knocked off the price. What you are telling the salesman is that you can afford the first $5600 of the cost of the car, but that the extra $50 will break your piggy bank. It just is not believable. A salesman who hears this will ignore it and hold out for his figures. Use "I cannot afford" for the monthly payment only. Approach the topic by telling the salesman that it is not just a few dollars a month, you have already stretched your budget allotment for a car by $20 a month and that is as far as you can possible go. Most salesmen can talk you into raising $5 on a monthly payment, but $25 a month is another matter.

When a salesman writes a deal and makes his presentation (offer) to you, never, ever, ask to use the restroom if you plan to negotiate the deal at all. That simple request will ruin any chance you may have had to work a better deal. If you have just returned from a 1-hour demonstration ride and are ready to sit down and talk business, now is the time to use the restroom. As soon as you sit down and begin to discuss figures, be prepared to sit there until you have the exact deal you want to sign. This may be a little more than difficult for someone with a bladder problem, but as soon as you head for the restroom the salesman will head for his sales manager to tell him to put a deal on the board. Here is why: For the most part, until the time you reach your final decision to buy, most every muscle in your body is tense. When you mentally reach a buy decision the salesman is not aware of it, but your body is. The figures satisfy you and so you relax. When you relax, your body functions go back to normal and what had been suppressed because of tension and anxiety now makes itself known. When you return to the negotiating table you may find the salesman insistent about the deal he is offering you.

BASIC RULES OF NEGOTIATION

Because the final price agreed upon will be somewhere between your opening bid (low) and his opening bid (high), start as close to dealer cost as possible, without going below it. Go too low and the salesman will suspect you are just guessing a deal. Go too high and you automatically lose money.

Whomever you negotiate with, you must remember never to come up on price faster than he comes down on price. If he is yielding in increments of $25 per offer, then you should yield $25 or less for each counteroffer. When a salesman moves only $25 per clip, he is trying to lead you to believe that he is close to his bottom figure; he must be because he can give you only another $25 on discount or trade allowance. His task is to keep the final figures as close to his opening offer as possible. The tactic is also designed to make you come up in leaps and bounds from your opening figure. You must convince the salesman that each offer of $25 you make could be your last offer—end of negotiating.

Never use the same number of dollars twice while making progressive offers; stagger the amounts as you increase your offers. If you consistently make offer after offer using increments of $25 on each increase, the salesman will spot this as a waiting game and simply begin to come down in smaller amounts, if he comes down at all. If he decides that you are using a program of increases, he must assume that there is no limit on the number of times you will come up on price. Use odd numbers for your increases: raise $25, then $32, then back to $25 again. Always go over $50 levels: Rather than an offer of $5250 make an offer of $5255; rather than $5300, make it $5312.

STRATEGIES

At some point in your negotiating the salesman will toss his pen on the desk and say, "Look, we are only $100 apart. Why don't we split the difference; I will come down $50 if you will come up $50." This is the greatest pick-me-up in the business. It usually gives the salesman the deal and an extra $50 more or less.

Normally, when a salesman wants to split the difference, he is just about ready to give you the deal you want and is merely trying to make a little more profit. When he wants to split the difference, get ready to hold to the last offer you made. If he will not come down to your figure, rather than split the difference with him, quarter it. If you are $100 apart, you will come up $25 and make him come down $75. When he sees he will not get the $50 he wants, he will take the $25.

A ploy frequently used by salesmen to gain an extra $50 to $100 on a deal is the break-even plea. The salesman assumes that you do not know dealer cost. The ploy is to convince you that your offer will put him in the hole or at best, give him a break-even deal. Therefore, you must pay a little more for your car. A used-car purchase is especially vulnerable to this tactic, for it is not possible to determine accurately just how much gross is in a particular car. A trade-involved deal is also susceptible because of the elusive true trade value. Caution is advised on a break-even plea. When in doubt, negotiate.

When a salesman writes a trade-involved deal for a new or used car, he must play down the trade-in and play up his car. He will usually itemize every feature of his car upon the face of the contract and will put only the year, model, and mileage of your car down for the trade information. The list on your trade-in will only be the reconditioning necessary to bring your car up to par. Although he originally inspected your car in silence, the salesman can now tear it apart by using the written word as his instrument—the ink on the paper, which has the quality of permanence and gives him the negotiating edge.

To offset this, list all the positive features of your trade-in when he swings the paper around for your signature. If he has listed reconditioning on your car, list whatever you found wrong with his car. If he stops you from itemizing, simply say, "That's all right; you took the time to list all the benefits of your car and I want to take the time to list those of my car."

When the deal is written, those items that are standard equipment from the factory need not be itemized on the contract. However, optional items should be itemized right on the face of the contract for your protection. If they are not on the contract, something may be missing when you take delivery, even if it was on the car when you inspected it and signed to buy it, and even if it was listed on the window sticker. Unless you paid full window-sticker price for the car, the dealer can always say that the discounted price you paid did not include the missing items. If you took delivery of the car, it implies that you accepted the car as equipped at that time.

Reasoning. Reasoning, in a negotiating situation, is nothing more than giving reasons why you feel as you do, why you think as you do, and why the other party should go along with you. Reasoning need not always be logical, valid, true, and accurate. It must make enough sense to convince the other person that unless he accepts what you are saying and makes a change, there will be no deal. As the customer, you must give the salesman reasons (stories, if necessary) that make enough sense to him so that he can go to his sales manager and convince him to make appropriate adjustments. It is not enough to sit there and obstinately demand more allowance or a larger discount; you need reasoning to win.

To talk up your car's trade value, choose from among the following:

1. "My car is a nice clean car that you will have no trouble selling for a nice clean profit."
2. "I could sell it myself for $500 more than you want to give me, but it would be an inconvenience for me to do so."
3. "I could sell my car at an auction for more than you want to give me."
4. "I cannot take that much of a loss on my car. You will have to come up on the trade allowance, which I am certain you can do."
5. "I have already been offered more for my car. I want to do business with your firm but you will have to come up a little before we can get together."
6. "I do not feel this is a fair deal to me. Why don't you sharpen up your pencil and do a little better?"

The salesman has his own set of reasoning tools, which make just enough sense to convince you that if you don't go along with him, there will be no deal. If he uses any of the following, ignore him:

1. "You are moving up 3 years for only X number of dollars. That is a fair deal for you." (Maybe it is and maybe it is not.)
2. "You do like my car (emotional involvement) and I can certainly use your trade-in (to make more profit), but you will have to come up on price."
3. "Here is the reconditioning we must do before we can sell your car for full retail." (The cost of reconditioning is passed on to the next buyer.)
4. "The average book value of your car is $X. (So who wrote the book?)
5. "I can buy the same car at the auction house for less than you want for your trade." (It is not the *same* car. Auction merchandise is always questionable in quality and origin.)
6. "My sales manager has years of experience. He feels your car is only worth $X. (It is only a feeling.)
7. "We are a very reasonable company. If we could do better, we would." (But if they can avoid doing better, they will.)

And so it goes, round for round. "If you must pay more for my product it is because I think my company is worth the extra money." (You are buying the product, not the company.) "We do a better job for you before and after the sale; service has to mean something, doesn't it?" (Why pay more for the same service someone else will get for paying less?) And you counterpropose: "Yes, but if you must allow me more for my trade-in it is because I think it is worth more. And besides, after I buy I will do everything I can to send you business by my personal recommendation. That has to mean something, doesn't it?" "We must get your car ready for our used car lot. Your car is in good shape, but we must take care of a few minor details." "If it is just a question of a few minor details, they can't cost that much to repair. There is nothing wrong with my car, and I have the receipts to show the tender loving care it received."

Disagree By Agreeing. A salesman knows that he must never argue with a customer, for he may win the argument and lose the sale. It is necessary for him to disagree by agreeing, which allows him to argue a point politely without offending the customer. All he must do is preface everything he is about to say with, "I agree with you completely, but I feel this way about it." Simply agree with him and give your side of the story: "I feel exactly the same way. However, I think it is possible that. . . ." "I agree with what you are saying, but here is how I feel about it."

The salesman may say, "My company must make a profit on this deal. You will have to come up to our price before we can deal." To which you counter, "I couldn't agree with you more. I realize your company must make a profit and, personally, I don't care how much profit you make—that's none of my business. But I have already gone over my limit, and I feel that my offer is fair to your company."

The Other Dealer's Price. It is impossible for any salesman to keep abreast of every model on the market, including all features, options, amenities, and changes, let alone sticker prices. What does this mean to you? If you are $100 apart on the deal, you can tell the salesman that you can get the same size car—or the same type of car—from Dealer X for $100 less than the price he proposes. The salesman wants to beat the other deal, if he can, rather than try to prove your credibility. Do not use the same product manufacturer for the comparison. Use a competitive manufacturer's product for price comparison (same basic model size and equipment).

Asking for Your Deal. Confidence in asking for a deal is best developed by lessening the degree of importance you attach to whether or not you get it. The more you want it, the harder it is to play your best hand and employ your best strategies.

Most people know they are to ask, but when the moment of truth arrives they become nervous, squirm in their seats, look down at the floor or up at the ceiling, and meekly ask for the deal. Salesmen know that a customer who asks for a deal meekly really expects to pay more and will oblige him and see that he does, in fact, pay more.

How you ask is very important. The question must be relaxed, as if you had just asked the salesman for a glass of water or a cup of coffee or a light for a cigarette. It must be done with confidence, as though you really expect to receive the deal and will be surprised if you do not. Do not mistake confidence for cockiness. To demand that the salesman give you the car for your price will only create a hostile, stubborn salesman.

Never hesitate to ask for a high trade allowance and discount. The worst that can happen is to be refused, and when you are refused you just give a little and ask again.

Deposits. To the dealership, a purchase agreement is not worth the paper it's written on if there is no deposit of value with it. A deposit can be cash, check, or the title to your trade-in. This indicates that, if the sales manager approves the deal as written and signed by you, you will consummate the purchase.

The question is, how much of a deposit do you need and in what form? A deposit should remain under your control, even though you give it to the salesman at the time you sign. If you give cash or the title to your car, the salesman controls the deposit. However, a salesman cannot cash a personal check immediately, and if necessary you can stop payment on it—therefore you control the deposit.

Your primary goal is to keep the deposit as low as possible. A salesman will ask for a deposit as soon as he thinks he has a deal going. Ask him how much he needs (not how much he wants, but how much he needs) and, regardless of his comments, tell him that you can give him a personal-check deposit for $25. If he asks for more, question his motives: "Why do you need more? What's wrong with twenty-five?" Give a salesman a $200-deposit and you can forget about changing your mind about the deal—you just bought. Always make the check payable to the dealership, never to the salesman.

MANAGEMENT DEAL APPROVAL

Few dealerships allow their salesman to write, negotiate, and finalize their own deals. Ninety-nine percent of the time a deal must be approved by upper management—either a sales manager, a general manager, or an officer of the company. Therefore, whatever a salesman offers or says to you is not binding on the dealership and means literally nothing without management approval. The salesman's job is to write a purchase commitment on your part and take it to management for approval or counteroffer.

Even though you are not dealing directly with the sales manager, your efforts must be just as strong as if you were face-to-face with him. Most salesmen relay your comments and objections to the sales manager just as you have expressed them.

Writing the Deal. When a salesman says, "Here is where I go to work for you," what he really is doing is preconditioning you. To precondition you, the salesman will assure you in the most soothing tones that he has your best interests at heart; that he really wants to see you get that new car; and that he will argue with his sales manager, if necessary, to see that you get a good deal. He will further precondition you to expect the worst possible. The lead-in goes like this: "I do not really think my sales manager will go along with this deal, but I will do my best to get it for you." Now you are set up for the refusal, and it will not be the salesman's fault when it comes.

Never, never tell a salesman your true bottom dollar, even if he is a relative. If his sales production and profit level is low for the month, you will become his high-profit sale for the month, simply because you trust him.

Never discuss your deal with whomever you may be sitting after the salesman leaves, and never divulge your bottom dollar when you think no one is listening. Although it is illegal, some dealers use listening devices, either transmitting bugs or land-line monitors, to listen to your conversation when the salesman is not there. If you want to discuss figures with someone, leave the closing room and talk elsewhere.

While your salesman is gone, you will be thinking, "Maybe I asked for too much. The salesman is probably right; I am a little too low on price. Well, I will go another $100 if his sales manager does not approve my offer. I sure do want that car; I can see it sitting in my driveway now. Wait until my next-door neighbors see this beauty. I wonder what's taking that salesman so long.'' And now you are ready for the salesman's return. Even though his sales manager can give him a yes or no in 60 seconds, you will not see your salesman for 15 minutes. If your salesman is to present the illusion of 15 minutes' effort fighting for your deal, he must be gone for 15 minutes. Another reason for his absence is to make you think that each time you make an offer, it will be 15 minutes before you get an answer on the deal. The first 15 minutes bothers no one; it is the second and third and fourth that begin to rattle the nerves. If your salesman takes too long to obtain a rejection, politely tell him that you do not plan to wait around all day each time he must go to management for a conference. ''Your sales manager knows whether he can sell me this car for my price or not, so see if you can make it a little quicker this time. I don't have all day to wait for your manager to make up his mind.'' Now he cannot play his little game, and he will return in 2 minutes with an answer. Your small display of impatience will also prompt them to give you the deal you want. (''He's getting ready to walk. Let's give him the car.'')

Here's what normally happens: the salesman takes your offer to his sales manager, quickly presents the deal, gives his opinion of the customer, and estimates how much more money he thinks he can make on the deal. The manager reviews the deal and writes a counteroffer. If the salesman needs advice or help on a specific problem, his manager will offer suggestions. After his manager scratches all over the contract and signs it, the salesman is ready to return and present the counteroffer.

When the salesman finally returns with the magic word, he will hold you in suspense for a moment. You are sitting there eagerly waiting to hear whether or not you own the car, and you want to see the contract. But first, it is story time. The salesman may lead in like this: ''Well, I did better than I expected. My sales manager could not give you the full trade value you wanted, but he did give you a fair trade figure (fair deal or good deal) based on current market conditions.'' (Wow, that's a relief to you and you have not even seen the deal yet.) He may ask, ''Do you want to take the car home with you today?'' which implies that he got the deal approved. You envision ownership—driving the car home, parking it in your driveway, and displaying it for all to see—all of which lowers your resistance to his counteroffer. Whatever he does say, it will be of a conciliatory nature.

Now he shows you the amended deal and asks for your acceptance. If you do not immediately accept, he will launch into the reasoning behind the counteroffer and again ask for an acceptance. Everything he says will be prefaced with assurances that he is doing the best he can for you.

You may see a lot of red-ink scribbling all over the revised contract that was so neat 15 minutes ago. This represents a red flag to you, for it means changes were made—changes not to your benefit. The purpose of the bright color and the abnormally large size of the figures is to draw your attention away from the deal as originally written and focus your attention on what the true deal is to be. However, do not become alarmed until you hear the salesman's beautifully told story.

If a trade-in is involved, the salesman will make his first reference to the numbers of the deal there. He must justify a lower allowance than you want. "If your car were in perfect condition, my manager could give you the allowance you want. However, as you know, your car needs some reconditioning to make it ready for our used-car lot; we cannot sell it as it sits. So, my manager had to deduct for reconditioning and get-ready charges" (get-ready charges that will be paid by the person who buys your old car). Ignore the deductions and get-ready charges and go back to your basic deal.

CounterOffer. The trade-involved counteroffer begins with a story. "Yes, my car does need some work to make it ready for resale. However, I did find a few things wrong with your car that I had not mentioned earlier. I really didn't want to be as picky as you seem to think you must be. Let's take another look at your car to be sure its condition is not as bad as you seem to think my car's is." (Dealing on a new car: "I did not like the ride; the engine idles rough; the steering pulls to one side. Let's take another drive. I'm not really sure I like it.") This approach is much better than trying to defend your car. You have ruined his procedure, ruined his ability to continue to pick your car apart, and you have put him on the defensive.

Go back to his car and begin your inspection all over again, or repeat the demonstration ride. Now the salesman will start to have second thoughts: maybe he and his sales manager should have taken your initial offer; maybe you will find more wrong with his car; maybe he will lose the deal altogether.

Rather than let you reinspect his car, the salesman may say, "Wait a minute; maybe I can get my sales manager to go along with your original offer." If he returns with his manager you know it is time for customer turnover; the salesman has used all his ammunition. If he returns alone with no deal approval, he has been instructed to continue to try to sell you.

While the salesman is gone, do not sit there and wait for his return. Go out onto the lot and check out his car again. If he obtains deal approval, he can bring it out to you. If it is turnover time, he must call you back to the closing room. If he brings a revised deal that you do not like, you are that much closer to leaving the dealership. The salesman wants you to stay in the closing room. If you wander off every time he leaves you alone, he will be that much quicker about returning and that much more nervous about losing you altogether.

Turnover. At any point, your salesman may elect to turn you over to his sales manager. Known as customer turnover, this technique is usually used only as a last resort effort to sell you. Turning you over to the manager brings fresh ideas to the closing table, as well as the manager's selling experience and expertise. It also brings a fresh, untired mind that will begin the negotiations as if nothing at all had happened thus far. You have become fatigued during the course of your negotiations and your resistance is lower than when you first began. The manager will usually begin at step one and duplicate the salesman's procedure. This ensures that points missed by the salesman are covered and further weakens your resistance to a point where you stop saying *no* and start saying *yes*. Persistence pays.

When you deal with the manager you will feel that when he makes you an offer it is truly the best that he can do. Don't believe it for a minute. The manager's job is to sell you a car, not to chase you out of the dealership. He must win you over, just as the salesman did, but in less time. He cannot take the chance that you will cool off. He may, however, become nasty when he finds out you are not going to buy. So be prepared to leave—quickly.

What works on the salesman works on the sales manager. He is a human being. But do not underestimate his abilities. He is a seasoned veteran in the automobile business. When facing the sales manager or a salesman who has made a counteroffer, you need a final set-up plan. This requires a believable story and a "nothing to lose" attitude.

You might say something like, "Mr. Salesman, I would really like to buy this car from you. You are the first salesman I have met with whom I would like to do business. Your company has a fine reputation, which I am sure will not disappoint me should we ever come to terms. Now, as much as I like the car, as much as I like you, and as much as I like your dealership, I do not feel that you are giving me your best deal possible. I'm quite sure you can do better."

Say nothing more and give the salesman a chance to make an incriminating commitment or statement. When you put it to him this way, there is nothing he can do except take your proposal to management and try for approval. If he returns with his manager for turnover, give him the same story. If he returns without approval of your deal, repeat the steps one more time: you like the car, you want to buy it from him, you have set a limit of how much you can spend, and you have reached your limit. Tell him how to contact you and begin to leave. As you are leaving, drop the hint that you will be buying from another dealer.

"Well, I guess I will have to buy from so-and-so down the street." This can be said to yourself, the salesman, or whomever might be with you—spouse, friend, or relative.

The following morning call the salesman and ask him whether he has had a chance to think about your offer. Repeat what you said the preceding day and tell him to check with his manager for a change of mind. Persistence pays, but there is a point at which it will do no good to ask one more time or a thousand more times. If the salesman still cannot—or will not—give you the deal you want, close with, "I just wanted to give you a chance to sell me a car before I go to another dealer and buy. I really like your car better."

If his response is an emphatic *no*, go elsewhere to buy or consider moving on price yourself. However, if you must spend more than originally planned, make the final decision to do so away from the influence of the dealer or salesman.

Supply and Demand Negotiating. When the supply of certain models is limited, negotiating is more difficult and consumer strategies are restricted. A limited supply can be caused by a popular model selling extremely well; by a factory withholding production to puff demand and restrict supply, or by a fuel shortage such as the ones that occurred in 1973 and 1979 which caused people to over-buy economy cars and created a general shortage. When the supply is low and demand high, dealers obstinately hold out for full window sticker price or very close to it. "If you don't buy it, someone else will," is the general attitude. So, when a dealer offers this lay-it-on-the-line statement, lay it on the line with him:

"Not if they have any sense they won't. Nobody pays full sticker price anymore. How long has that car been sitting on your lot, anyway? I'm offering you a sale right now. When is that someone else going to come along? Are you going to be the salesman who sells it to that someone else or is another salesman going to get the commission? I have the time to wait. There are other economy cars on the market and most other dealers are a little more reasonable than you seem to want to be.'' Or you might say ''The car is four months old and you expect me to pay the full price for it? I'm going to get eight months use for one year's depreciation. No way. You have discounted this model for other people I have talked to, and that was several months ago. And now, when the model is older, you expect me to pay more.''

NEGOTIATING SYNOPSIS

1. Someone must make an initial offer. The salesman will normally solicit your bid to him. If you insist that he make you an offer, it will be a token discount to start the negotiations.
2. The salesman's opening offer will be very close to sticker price; so your first offer should be very close to dealer cost.
3. Never come up on price faster than the salesman comes down.
4. The salesman will do as much verbal negotiating as possible. It is easier for him to raise you on price verbally than in writing.
5. The time lag between showing the written figures and getting your signature will be kept minimal by the salesman to decrease the time you have to think about those figures. Take your time before signing, regardless of the salesman's urging.
6. The salesman will seek a commitment to purchase from you each time he makes a lower offer. You must seek a commitment from him to accept your offer each time you raise your offer to him.
7. Everything the salesman does is subject to management approval; everything you do is binding. You must therefore convince the salesman to take an offer to management as soon as possible to discover management thinking about price, discount, and trade allowance.
8. Negotiating with management involves leg work by the salesman, and several rounds of offer and counteroffer. At about the third or fourth round of negotiations, management will have made about its best offer to you. This does not mean you should quit negotiating, but that you are getting close.
9. Continued negotiating is always possible, provided you continue to come up on your price. If you freeze your figure, management may also pick a point and freeze. Raise by some amount, if it is only $5.
10. Don't display excitement; avoid exclamations such as: ''We just

have to have that car! I've wanted a car like this for years! I can't wait to show this off to the neighborhood! Wow, what a terrific car!'' It is deadly to your deal to show excitement about the car.

OFFER AND COUNTEROFFER PROCEDURE AND DIALOGUE

The salesman's offer to you: "I can sell you this car," or, "You can buy this car for $4,500 and your car in trade. How does that sound?"

Your counteroffer: "Well, I had a different figure in mind. I am thinking of a $4,000 cash difference—$4,000 and my car in trade. How about it?"

His objection or protest: "No, there is no way we can go that low."

Your response: "Is it that you *cannot* meet my price or that you *will* not meet it?" (Wait for an answer.)

"Mr. Customer, at that price we will make no money. My manager would never go along with that deal. Your car in trade, and $4,500 is a fair deal to you. What do you think? Do you want to pick the car up tomorrow or do you want to take it home with you today?"

"Mr. Salesman, if you cannot let me have the car for $4,000 and my car in trade, just how close can you come to my figure?"

"I might be able to come down a little, but I would really be surprised if I could get my manager to go along with it. We are not making much profit at $4,500. Will you buy the car if I can get my manager to go along with a $4,450 cash difference?"

Now you can either counteroffer or take another look at his car.

"Mr. Salesman, before I consider spending a dollar more than $4,000, I will have to take another look at your car. I am already several hundred dollars over my limit, but I do like your car—sort of. Let's go look it over and see if it is really worth the money."

Now reinspect the car entirely, front to back, complete with another demonstration ride. "Can we take it for another ride—there was something about the way it handled the first time I drove it that I didn't like."

Back in the closing room: "Well, Mr. Salesman. To me, $4,000 still seems like a reasonable figure, but if you want more money, I guess I could come up to $4,050. If you will give me the car for $4,050, I'll take it."

"Mr. Customer, I just cannot sell the car for that low a price. Let me write it up for $4,400 and your car and see whether I can get my manager to approve it."

"Since the final approval rests on your sales manager, take him my offer of $4,075 and let him decide."

The salesman may ask you to justify your figure. Now is a good time to tell him about the car you can get for less from another dealer.

"Mr. Customer, if another dealer will sell it to you for less, why don't you buy from him?"

"Well, the price is right, but I prefer the color of your car more than the other. However, I do not plan to spend more than $4,100 for the sake of color. Write it up, and when your manager approves it I can take the car home today. I am ready to do business."

Use time to your advantage: "I am ready to buy today, but I'm not going to throw money away. I can wait to buy the car; there is no hurry."

Be prepared for customer turnover at any time. Relax when it happens.

Let them invest time in you. The more time invested, the less they will want to lose you and the sale. Demonstration rides and inspections are great time consumers.

Let them know that you can find another dealer faster than they can find another customer.

Frequently use the negative notes you took during inspection and demonstration rides.

Frequently use the "sound of silence." Just because the salesman or his manager asks a quick question does not mean you must give a quick answer.

TEN-STEP PROGRAM TO BUY A CAR

1. **Research.** Know what your car is worth, know which cars are on the market, be aware of financing rates and monthly payments.
2. **Know Exactly What You Want.** Sit down and list your wants, needs, preferred model, and desired equipment. Stick to this list except for small items you may have initially overlooked; make no major changes in plans once you begin to look. Determine exactly what you can afford and for how long.
3. **Be Prepared to Shop.** Even though you are knowledgeable about dealer cost and what constitutes a good deal, you may have to shop to find the dealer willing to give you the deal you want.
4. **Do What the Salesman Does.** If he smiles, smile. If he slams the door of your car, slam the door of his car. If he is argumentative, be argumentative. If he asks questions of you, ask them of him. If he is quiet (or loud), be quiet (or loud).
5. **Inspect Your Merchandise.** Always inspect the very same car you plan to buy; never inspect a similar car on the assumption that similar is equal. Inspect methodically and thoroughly; cover

every square inch of the car you plan to buy—new or used.

6. **Negotiate Wisely.** Be emotionally detached from your purchase. When you talk dollars and cents, do not let a pretty color or gingerbread extras influence your final decision.

7. **Write the Deal You Want.** Control the writing of the deal, for this is money out of your pocket. If a salesman will not at least write an offer to submit to upper management, leave the dealership.

8. **Handle the Salesman's Objections.** Be prepared to handle the salesman when he talks higher price or lower trade allowance. Justify your position, present your evidence, utilize your strategies.

9. **Do not exceed Preset Limits.** It does little good to set limits if you can be talked into going over them. Never exceed preset limits without first sleeping on it. Wait one full day before making a final decision.

10. **Double-Check Everything.** Double-check all figures and paperwork—particularly financing papers—and be certain you know exactly what you are receiving and that everything matches what you and the dealer have agreed upon. Reinspect the car you are buying before you take delivery and ownership.

10
Buying a Used Car

THE USED CAR

IF YOU WANT TO BUY a used car, the rules of the game are shop, look, and be patient. You may have to shop twelve to fifteen used-car dealers to get a good car and a good deal. Once you have decided on make, model, year, and price range, you must then go out and find them.

You cannot figure dealer cost on a used car (although there are guidelines to help), so value and cost are elusive. No two cars will be in the same condition, so a careful inspection is mandatory. You will hear unbelievable stories, meet some crazy salesmen, and see tricks that put magicians to shame. But it can be fun.

The statement, "Buying a used car is buying someone else's troubles," is illogical logic, yet the fear of used merchandise persists in the mind of the consumer. If you can believe the fact that not everyone trades in a car just because it is giving him trouble, you will find it easier to make your purchase. Consider, too, that you always have the right to thoroughly inspect the car, drive it, and have it checked out by a mechanic and, when you are certain that it is mechanically fit, you have the right to buy and enjoy it.

Price Tags. There are two major reasons you will not find price tags on most used cars on most lots. The first and most obvious reason is that the tactic forces you to stop and ask a salesman the price of a particular car. The second, and less obvious, reason is that it permits the salesman to juggle his price according to what he sees and hears.

A used-car salesman will rarely start quoting prices until he determines what you have on your mind. He must know the type of buyer you are and what your buying habits are before he begins to make commitments. Are you a trade value buyer, a cash difference buyer, an original purchase price buyer, or a monthly payment buyer? What is important to you? What makes you buy a car? When he has the answers to these questions, he will tailor the deal to best satisfy your buying habits, tell you what you want to hear, and show you what you want to see.

The Monthly Payment Shuffle. By questioning you, a salesman discovers whether he should show you a low purchase price, although it means showing you a low trade allowance, or show you a high trade allowance, although it means puffing the prices of his cars. Ideally, for the salesman, you will give him a monthly payment ceiling. By working backward on his figures, he can compute how much money your monthly payment will buy.

Say you want a monthly payment of $100. He drops back to $90 a month, which will buy about $3,000 spendable cash. He now adds his pack (say, $400) and your trade value ($400), which brings the total to $3,800. He now knows that he will be quoting you $3,800, and that he can allow you up to $800 for your trade-in on any given car and the monthly payment will work out to $90, or $10 less than you said you wanted to spend. He can now show you anything he has in stock in which he has invested no more than $3,000 and make a profit on the sale. He may have only $2,000 invested in a particular car, but he will still quote you $3,800 and allow you $800 trade allowance, because the final figure will be within your affordable monthly payment range.

The Fixed-Dollar Shuffle. Giving a salesman a fixed number of dollars you can spend is just as bad as giving him a monthly payment. Suppose you tell him you can spend $2,000. Naturally, everything he shows you will be priced at about $2,000, because that is what you told him you wanted—a $2,000 price tag. But among the several cars he points out will be one or two that he would normally sell for $1,500 to $1,600. The price goes up when you tip your hand.

When a salesman asks for a price range or how much you want to spend per month, tell him that you are flexible on purchase price and that the monthly payment will depend upon the car you finally choose to buy. Tell him also that what you buy depends in large part upon how good the deal is. If you give him figures, make it a spread: ''I am thinking of something between $80 and $110 a month (or $2,500 and $3,000). Naturally, I do not want to go all the way up to a $110 payment, but I will if the car is nice enough and the deal is good enough." Now the salesman has a benchmark from which to work, but he has neither a firm commitment nor firm numbers with which to put phony figures together.

Model Selection. Do not request specific brand names; ask for general categories—compact, intermediate, full-size. If you ask for a Brand A compact and he has Brands A, B, and C, the salesman will hold out for a higher price on the Brand A because he knows you want it. "I could give you the B or C for $2,500, but I have to get at least $2,800 for that Brand A. And it's a great car, popular too. Everybody's looking for a Brand A these days." If he has several compacts on his lot, treat the one you want with indifference; use one car against the other.

Even though you may prefer a Brand A, you may find another brand name in the same category at a better price and in better condition. Be flexible and open-minded. The more cars you are willing to look at, the larger your market.

USED-CAR INSPECTION

The inspection of a used car is extremely important, for even if the price is fantastically low it means nothing if you must pay for major repairs or if the car suffers a thousand nickle-and-dime ailments after warranty expiration.

Inspecting a used car is simple—start at the front bumper and check everything from there on back. When you reach the rear bumper you are finished. Some people do it in 5 seconds. These quick inspections create many problems that usually develop after you take ownership.

You need not be a registered mechanic to inspect a car. All it takes is a system to follow so that nothing is overlooked. There are two phases: the physical inspection performed on the lot, and the demonstration ride. During the physical inspection, there are four areas to check: body and attached parts, engine and fluid levels, interior components, and switches that turn on and off. To begin your inspection you must adopt an attitude that leaves nothing to assumption. Just because it is there does not mean it works. The first time you break the rule, it will be on the one item that does not work.

Area One: Body and Attached Parts. Always inspect the body of a car in daylight. Wrinkles, body work, fading and mismatched paint, and small rust spots and scratches are all fairly well hidden or disguised at night regardless of the artificial lighting on the lot. From the front bumper, driver's side, begin a slow walk around the car and let your eyes cover every square inch of the body. When you find a blemish, touch it, but do not comment to the salesman and be certain that he sees you touch it. He knows that you know, but he does not know what you are thinking. When you have finished the walk, stand back 5 to 10 feet and check the car for paint mismatch—one part that is a shade lighter or darker than another part. Do this on both sides, and on the front and back. Mismatch does not automatically spell accident, for even new cars occasionally have mismatched paint, but it is cause for further investigation. Overspray, strong paint mismatch, and/or sanding grooves on doorjambs, inside the hood, and inside the trunk compartment will really tell whether major body work has been done.

Stand at the front and then at the rear of the car and sightline the body. All lines should run together smoothly; a major style line that runs the full length of the car should be straight all the way. Any unusual bulges in the body indicate that patch work has been done. Check suspect areas with a small magnet. The thicker the body putty, the more easily the magnet will slide off. Move the magnet around until you have a feel for what is good metal and what is body putty. This little test will tell you what is under the paint and the size of the repair. The larger the area of body putty, the shoddier the work, and the more likely that problems will develop in the future.

If the car has a vinyl or convertible top, check the top for fit, tears, and slits. Tops shrink, so check to see whether it has pulled loose at the edges. A convertible rear window should be clear and preferably of glass. Bubbles on vinyl tops indicate rusting beneath, which is expensive to remedy.

Bumpers that show signs of rust are on their way out. This situation will get progressively worse as the rust works its way under the good chrome, loosens it, and lifts it off by blistering and peeling. A dented bumper cannot be restored to its original condition without rechroming, which is expensive. All chrome should fit snugly against the body of the car and align properly. Gaps between chrome and body collect dirt and moisture, which will eventually cause rust. A side-view mirror that shows black spots behind the glass is just about shot.

Tires should match by brand name and by tire tread depth. If all four are not the same, they should at least match by pairs (front two or back two). Be sure you can tell the difference between glass-belted, steel-belted, and radial steel-belted tires. A dealer may let some air out of all four tires to give them that flattened, radial look. Read the raised print on the side of the tire. When in doubt, have the kind of tire spelled out on the purchase contract.

Area Two: Engine and Fluid Levels. Inspect the engine compartment from front to rear, beginning with the radiator. Twist the cap off and check the fluid level and color. Sealed and semiclosed cooling systems are exempt from this check. If the coolant is a muddy-looking, rusty color, the engine and radiator need to be flushed and cleaned (relatively inexpensive but a good negotiating point). Run your finger around the inside and underside of the radiator opening. The fluid may look clean only because it was recently changed with fresh water and antifreeze added. A residue is usually left behind at this spot. Be certain that the salesman sees the residue (if any) and remember it when you negotiate.

Next is the fan blade and belt. Grab the top blade and wiggle it back and forth, first toward the engine block and then toward the radiator. There should be a little give when you do this, but too much wiggle indicates that the water pump shaft bearing is bad or is going bad. Caution is advised. (Electric fans are exempt. When you start the engine, the fan will not begin to operate immediately. Most are thermostatically controlled and function only when the engine reaches operating temperature.) Check the fan belt for cracks and wear and tear. Twist it around at various spots and check the underside (the side against the pulleys). A shiny look or deep cracks indicate that replacement is needed.

Twist the oil cap off and inspect. A filthy cap indicates a lack of proper maintenance. Check the oil dipstick for fluid level and color. If it is a quart low, you do not know how many miles made it a quart low (once around the block?). All oil turns a faint brown when exposed to engine heat. However, if the dipstick shows black oil, then the oil and the oil filter need replacement. Rub some oil between thumb and forefinger. If it is gritty with a substance like fine sand, caution is advised. That grit could be fine metal granules, indicating internal engine problems, or dirt from improper maintenance.

Take the cover off the air cleaner (wing nut) and check the air filter. When it is held up to a strong light or direct sunlight, some light should filter through. If it is filthy, it should be replaced. Push open the butterfly (a flat piece of metal within the throat of the carburetor) and look down into the throat. If it is black and sooty, that indicates a lack of proper maintenance, a bad air cleaner, cheap fuel usage, or backfiring through the carburetor. This is a good negotiating point, and a spray can of carbuertor cleaner will make it shine like new. (Some dealers bolt the air cleaner on so it cannot be removed. Do not buy the car until you have inspected the carburetor with the air cleaner off.)

Take all caps off the battery and check the fluid levels. (Fully sealed batteries with no caps are exempt.) All cells should be at their proper levels. A cell low on fluid could be a bad cell, indicating that the entire battery is going bad. All cells must be functional for the battery to work it all. Batteries are not cheap.

Optional power equipment gives you more fluid levels to check: power steering fluid, brake fluid, and the air-conditioning system. Small white spots—usually a white, powdery residue—on and around the air-conditioning compressor indicate that Freon (Tm) gas has escaped.

If you notice fresh electrical tape anywhere on the car it indicates recent electrical problems. Check extra carefully; ask questions. The real test of the electrical system is when you check switches that turn on and off.

Check for oil seepage around the engine block. Fresh oil running down the side of the engine block indicates that a gasket must be replaced. The gasket is inexpensive, but the cost of labor is high.

If you have a friend who is a mechanic, have him check the car for you for a small fee, or take it to any private garage and, for a nominal fee, have it inspected. Have the following items checked: the compression, the coolant for antifreeze and degree of protection, battery efficiency, brake linings, and transmission. Do not accept a recent state, county, or city inspection sticker as valid evidence of the car's reliability. The dealer may have a friend who will put a sticker on any car regardless of condition and without a full inspection.

Area Three: Interior Components. If the seats are not missing, the steering wheel is in place, and there are pedals on the floor, all seems to be in order. Not quite. Inspect the full length of the front seat before you sit down. Tears and holes become worse with use and are very costly to repair. Look straight up and inspect the headliner, sunvisors, and dome light for damage. Check the rear seat for damage and/or stains. This is where kids usually sit and do their thing of spilling fluids. The older the car and the lower the price, the less fussy you need be about small stains.

Check all door handles and window crank handles. Crank all windows fully up and down and back up again. If a window catches, sticks, or takes a sudden drop, it may be that there is a bad gear or the window is ready to fall off the track. On power windows, be certain that each individual switch by each window is functional. The master switch by the driver's seat might work on all windows, but an individual switch may be bad—they are expensive.

Check carpeting for tears, holes, and pulling away from edges clamped down. If there are floor mats, lift them up and check the condition of the floor or carpet underneath. No carpet? Check the metal floor for rusting.

Inspect the glove box, open and close it; lock and unlock it. On a remote-control mirror, check to be sure the inside knob is actually connected, and that it works. Check the seat back release on two-door models, and the forward and backward slide of the front seat. Check all locks on all doors, inside with the knob and outside with the key. Seat belts should be functional. If they are of the self-returning reel type they should operate smoothly but, most important, they should operate.

Check the trunk for a spare tire and jack, naturally. If one or the other is missing, insist it be included. Lift the mat or carpet covering the floor of the trunk and check for rusting. Check both side wells for rust and/or body work.

Area Four: Switches That Turn On and Off. Check the mileage first. Twelve thousand miles per year of age is considered normal. It is difficult, even for an expert, to determine whether the odometer has been turned back on any given car. Mileage statement forms are misleading, since many people sign them blank when they trade their car. If there is an oil change sticker on the doorjamb or under the hood, check it against the odometer reading. In the final analysis, it is best to forget the possibility of mileage tampering and concentrate instead on the inspection and your own personal opinion of the condition of the car.

Begin on the driver's side, extreme left, and check everything that pulls, pushes, or switches on and off. Put the emergency brake on and pull the knob to release it. Some models have an automatic emergency brake release that kicks out when the car is placed in gear. Check the headlight switch, bright beam and low beam, dashboard dimmer, and interior dome light switch. With someone standing outside the car, check the left and right turn signals, front and rear; check the horn (the most commonly overlooked item); hit the brakes and be certain the lights work on both sides.

It is best to check windshield wipers from inside. Check that the motor works, the washer fluid squirts, and the wipers clear the windshield properly for a clear field of vision. Bad blades leave wide streaks.

Check heater and air-conditioner during the demonstration ride. A cold engine will throw no heat. In the winter it will be necessary to pull the car indoors to check the air-conditioner. As a precaution, add a conditional clause to your purchase contract: "Air-conditioner will be fixed by dealer, with no charge to customer, if it fails to work when summer arrives."

Check all functions of the radio—AM/FM—to be certain all work. On a tape player, either built in or added on, play a tape all the way through.

Be wary of add-on equipment such as an air-conditioning unit. It might work now, it might work forever, but who knows. Do not assume that just because a clock is present, it works. Car clocks are notorious for not working. Check the cigar lighter and all miscellaneous lights: glove box, ashtray, light groups, and trunk light.

Luxury cars usually have extras such as a tilt steering wheel, speed control, automatic trunk release, power seats, power door locks, and power antenna, all of which should work. Check a power sun roof several times for seal and functional operation. If possible, run the car through a jet-spray car wash to check for leaks everywhere—windows, trunk, sunroof, moonroof.

Put the top of a convertible down and up several times. Many times the motor has the ability to put the top down but cannot quite make it come back up. If the motor is weak or if the hydraulic lines are low on fluid, you will have a problem.

Check the rear window of a station wagon, if it is power operated, to be certain it works both with the switch on the dashboard and with the key in the rear door. Work fold-down seats up and down, and check for looseness and fit. Check the luggage rack for looseness and rattles, rusting and/or pitting. Check woodgrain sidepanels for general condition—discoloration (sun bleaching), and nicks, tears, bubbles, or other damage. Sidepanels cannot be patched and they are expensive to replace.

The effect that rust and blemishes or any other malfunctions on the car have on your final decision depends on the severity of the problems, the price versus the age of the car, and your own personal judgment. The final, bottom-line judgment of value depends upon how one car compares to everything else you have seen. Does the general physical condition justify the price?

If by this time the car checks out and you are interested in it, you are ready for the demonstration ride. The demo ride should follow the physical inspection, never precede it. If the car does not check out, you will have wasted the demo ride and your time. Also, if the engine is operated for several minutes, it disturbs the fluid levels and makes the radiator too hot to check.

Start the engine, put the emergency brake on, and place the transmission in a forward gear. (For Standard shift, place in first gear—clutch pedal depressed.) Give it a little gas (release the clutch pedal slowly) to test the holding power of the emergency brake. (Automatic brake release does not apply here. It will have to be checked on a steep hill with the brake on, the engine off, and the transmission in neutral.) Listen to the muffler system with your door open, preferably between two other cars. Become familiar with all controls and pedal locations and drive away.

Most salesmen have a planned route on which they take their customers, that usually includes hills, city traffic, and highway driving to give them a good profile of what the car can do. You will want a little more from a demo ride than the salesman's route to help you decide. Take the car home and then drive it from there to your place of employment so you will know how it takes the bumps and driving conditions of your normal daily route. If the test drive over that route presents problems, forget that car. If your drive to work does not include hills and highways, find them on your way back to the dealership; check the car under all driving conditions when possible. Utilize all your senses: Listen for any unusual noises; feel for any vibrations in the steering wheel, poor shock absorption on bumps, drift or pull in steering to one side of the road; and keep an eye on all gauges—temp, oil, amp.

When you return to the dealership, check the fluid levels of the power steering unit and the power brakes again. If there is a loss of fluid from your short trip, the unit will have to replaced. The dealer may add fluid as necessary to maintain the fluid level and keep the defective unit working until the car is sold. Thereafter, you will be on your own. Also listen for any hissing noises, such as steam escaping. Some defects do not show up until the engine reaches operating temperature. Check the oil dipstick for oil level, and look under the car for oil leakage.

Inspection Do's and Dont's. Do not slam the doors, trunk lid, or hood of the car unless that is the only way you can get the part to stay closed. This shows a complete lack of concern for something that isn't yours and will not necessarily prove any part to be defective.

Do not redline the engine. This is flooring the accelerator and holding it to the floor while the engine races at full speed, transmission in neutral. Gunning the engine proves nothing more than the ignorance of the person doing it. If you do not blow out the engine, you may cause internal damage that will not appear until months after you buy the car. And you will have to pay for the repairs.

Do not kick the tires as you make your rounds of the car. There is too much weight on each tire for you to be able to tell anything by kicking them. Kicking tires does not harm the car, but it tells the salesman that you are putting on a show as if to say, "I am no dummy when it comes to inspecting a car."

Do not refer to a salesman's merchandise as junk. Customers do this because they think it gives them negotiating leverage—it does not. Never tell a salesman how to run his lot or that he should fix this or that. Do not pick apart every car on his lot, only the one you plan to buy. Criticizing every car will create defensive resistance in the salesman, which will surface when you sit down to negotiate the deal.

Treat the car you inspect as if you owned it, and as you would want someone else to treat your car. Before the day's end it might be your car.

Do take notes on everything as you go along.

Do take your time; be thorough. If the salesman rushes you, slow him down.

Do not hesitate to ask any question—you will not embarrass the salesman.

Inspection Checklist

Rate each block E (Excellent), G(Good), F(Fair), P(Poor)

	CAR: 1	2	3	4	5	6	7
Area One: Body and attached parts.							
Wrinkles, body work, and rust							
Sightline for style line continuity							
Vinyl top for tearing and bubbles							
Bumpers for pitting, and general condition							
Tires for match and tread depth							

CAR:

	1	2	3	4	5	6	7

Area Two: Engine and Fluid Levels.

Radiator for fluid level and color
Fan blade and belts for wear and fit
Oil dipstick for level and color
Power steering/brake fluid levels
Air cleaner/filter for cleanliness
Air-conditioning system for leaks
Fresh electrical tape
Oil/fluid seepage around engine block

Area Three: Interior Components.

All upholstery, headliner, and carpets
All door handles and window cranks
Glove box, remote-control items
Trunk for spare tire and jack, and for rust

Area Four: Switches That Turn On and Off

Headlights, interior lights
Emergency brake—on and off
Turn signals, brake lights, horn
Windshield wipers and washer fluid
Heater and air-conditioner functions
All functions of radio/tape player

Special Areas.

Add-ons: air-conditioning and tow equipment
Clock, cigar lighter, gauges
Miscellaneous light groups
Tilt steering wheel, speed control
Power seats, windows, and door locks
Top up-and-down on convertible
Rear window and folding seats on station wagon
Luggage rack and woodgrain siding

THE PREVIOUS OWNER

Ever hear of the little old lady who drove her car only 14 miles on Sunday to and from church, and a few miles during the week for shopping and socials? This used to be a good selling point and almost guaranteed a sale when a salesman could prove it was true. Long ago, a low-mileage car was considered a better buy than one with high mileage. It is now known that the worst type of driving you can do is short runs, which actually cause more problems than long-distance driving.

Short runs do not let the engine reach peak operating efficiency. They waste more fuel and, over a period of time, cause carbon build-up that congests the engine. If you are considering two cars—both of the same year, make, and model—and one has higher mileage, the low-mileage car will not necessarily be the better buy. Such information as the previous owner's occupation, the car's major usage, and its maintenance history will tell more than the mileage.

When possible, call the previous owner and get the answers you need (including the kind of gas mileage the car was getting). Also find out what he bought and how he feels about the dealership—whether they have been fair with him, whether he is happy with his new car and the service obtained.

In the final analysis, the car will speak for itself. A good showing on a thorough inspection and good performance during the demo ride are the major criteria. And, of course, the price must be right.

Before you reject a car for having too many small things wrong with it, consider that even though it may have ten (or even twenty) flaws, the balance of the several thousand component parts are good. The real question is: What will it cost to fix the flaws and who will be paying for it? If it is a major component—engine or transmission—the dealer will surely have to make the repair or replacement. The first step is to itemize exactly what is wrong with the car and work from your list, both to reach a buy decision and to negotiate.

If your list contains mostly inexpensive repairs and replacements, consider fixing them yourself for the sake of being able to work a better deal. Ask the salesman how much of your list he will fix and let him obligate himself before the papers are drawn for you to sign. Point out that his car has a long list of flaws but that a good price will offset the small items. "I don't mind if the cigar lighter doesn't work, but the price must be right. Here is what is wrong with the car (go over your list with him). Now, give me the car for this price and fix the radio, and I will take care of the other repairs myself. How about it? Is it a deal?''

The longer the list, the greater your negotiating strength. This is why it is so important to do a thorough job of your initial inspection of the car.

Your guideline: If you plan to take care of the small items, negotiate the major items as part of the original deal and make your offer to the salesman. If you plan to have the dealer take care of your entire list, negotiate the best cash deal possible and then present your list, however long it might be, as a condition of your purchase.

USED-CAR WARRANTY

A warranty, in essence, is a courtesy to the customer and an inducement to buy. It satisfies the psychological fear, ''What if something happens when I drive the car off the lot?''

A warranty must cost someone money, for nothing is free. The longer a warranty runs, and the more areas of the car it covers, the higher the dealer's profit must be. A car that carries a 90-day, 100 percent warranty must cost more than a car that carries a 30-day, 50/50 warranty. The probability of something's going wrong within 90 days is four to five times greater than the probability of its occurring within 30 days. You pay extra for this higher probability, and for this (sometimes illusionary) security and protection. Before you begin to negotiate your deal, decide whether you want a better price or a better warranty.

Instead of a dealer-backed warranty, consider creating your own warranty or repair fund to cover repairs during your first few months of ownership. This gives you negotiating leverage when all other cards have been played. To use this leverage, you must first negotiate the dealer down to his lowest acceptable price and reserve your no-warranty offer until last. You must also determine optimum warranty value—the value of the projected repairs that this particular car will need during normal warranty coverage. You must look at it as the dealer does: ''What could go wrong with this car in a given length of time and how much will it cost to fix or replace it?'' A good rule of thumb is $50 per month of warranty coverage (computed against the dealer's warranty offer) or $50 per year of age of the car you plan to buy. This means that a dealer who offers a 6-month warranty is, in all probability, holding back $300 to pay for necessary warranty repairs. If the car has only a 1-month warranty, use the age of the car to compute optimum warranty value. A 1-year old car will compute to only $50, but it is reasonable to expect that that is all the car needs during your first year of ownership. However, a 4-year-old car will compute to $200 warranty valuation, which is reasonable to expect during the first year of ownership.

When you have negotiated the dealer's bottom-dollar price, make an "as is," no-warranty offer for the car. This is aside from any defects discovered during your inspection that the dealer has agreed to fix. An "as is" offer means that you are willing to take the car as it sits, except for any negotiated repairs. Your "as is" offer will be the salesman's bottom price less the optimum warranty value you have computed. If he will not agree to your offer, ask him how much lower he will go on an "as is" purchase. If it is a reasonable reduction of price, give it consideration. But the value must be there for you to take the chance.

USED-CAR VALUATION

What is the value of a used car? How is value determined?

The value of any car, very simply put, is whatever you, the buyer, are willing to pay for it and whatever price the seller is willing to take for it.

A salesman may call upon evidence to justify value, such as his Blue Book, normal market averages for a particular car, ads in the newspaper, and recent previous sales of the same or very similar merchandise. Point out to him that all this means nothing to you and that you will determine value on the individual merits of the car itself. You then offset his persistence that the value of the car is as he says.

A common sales tactic to justify value is to describe all the work done to the car to make it just the right, problem-free car for you. This is illusion. When the salesman rattles off a list of everything that has been done, consider that it may or may not be true. His dealership might have done the work, as he says, or it might have been done by the previous owner. If the car needed repairs and if the dealer did, in fact, make the repairs, he did not invest his own money on them—he invested the previous owner's money by underallowing for the trade-in.

When the salesman offers a lit, say, "The car must have been in pretty poor condition to need all that work. What else is wrong with it that you did not fix?" Or act shocked: "It needed all of that? Maybe I had better look at something a little less abused."

Your benchmark to negotiate a deal on any used car is to start with the wholesale value, or less, and work up from there, since the dealer is going to start from as high as he can and work down. Here are basic guidelines:

1. Compute the depreciated value of the car—wholesale and retail. Assume that the wholesale figure you derive is the maximum amount the dealer allowed the previous owner. More probably it was less.
2. Find out what the previous owner bought; for what new car did he trade?
3. Always assume the dealer has at least a $700 profit built into the price he quotes. From that point adjust your figures according to what the previous owner bought. The following examples help determine at what amount to begin your negotiations.

Example A:	Selling price of car:	$3,500
	Assumed profit level:	−$ 700
	Opening figure to begin negotiating:	$2,800
Example B:	Selling price of car:	$3,500
	Average wholesale price of car:	$3,500
	Customer bought $8,000 full-size car; 21% factor; $1,600 play money (packing). Profit held on new car sale:	$ 600
	Presumed allowance to customer:	$3,500
	$1,000 used to pack trade-in:	− $1,000
	Theoretical cash in trade-in:	$2,500

Here you must second-guess the dealer. Assume first that there is at least the $700 profit level within the car to utilize as negotiating money. Accept as a well-established fact that the dealer will not give a salesman any more of the gross than absolutely necessary to keep him happy. On the higher priced, full-size merchandise, a salesman will usually be content to go along with the dealer and accept a $600 or $800 gross on a deal, especially if the dealer insists that he go along with it. So the salesman's loss can be your gain if you know what the prior owner bought. That portion of the available gross that was used to pack the trade brings the dealer's total investment in the trade-in down. In the above examples it would be safe to use a $2,500 to $2,800 opening figure to begin the negotiations, even though the car's wholesale valuation is $3,000. Your concern is not what the car should sell for wholesale or retail, but rather for how much it can be purchased, which is based on how much the dealer has invested.

Example C:

Selling price of car:	$3,500
Average wholesale price of car:	$3,000
Customer bought $5,500 mid size	
car; 17% factor; $935	
play money. Profit held:	$ 435
Presumed allowance to customer	$3,300
$ 500 used to pack trade-in:	− $ 500
Theoretical cash in trade-in:	$2,800

An intermediate car allows the dealer room to negotiate and play with the trade-in figures, but not as much as the full-size car. The dealer will again try to book the car for as little as possible and still keep the salesman happy. A $435 gross pays the salesman $109 (25 percent of gross), which is reasonable.

In the above example you would be safe to use a $2,800 to $2,900 opening negotiating figure. You will fall within the built-in $700 profit level at $2,800. It is safe to assume that the dealer held a profit on the new car sale of about $400, and that the dealer did not allow full retail for the customer's trade, nor was he able to get away with showing him a wholesale figure. The allowance given for the trade had to be somewhere between wholesale and retail; thus, $3,300 was the trade allowance.

If the previous owner bought a compact, the gross involved is initially so small that the salesman must work extremely close on the deal. He cannot pack the trade-in nearly as well as he can on a full-size or inter-mediate purchase. The dealership will look very closely at the trade-in before even allowing wholesale for it. The slightest mistake in judgment could wipe out the entire profit made on the sale. On a compact deal, it is best to assume that the dealer held a $300 to $400 gross profit, and that any overage was used to pack the trade allowance. And there is always the $700 profit level to work with.

THE USED-CAR DEAL

Some salesmen work a deal by trading on terminology—trading retail to retail or wholesale to wholesale. In essence, the salesman is telling you that if you want full retail for your trade-in you must pay full retail for his car. Conversely, if you are to buy his car for wholesale, you must accept wholesale for your car. When a salesman begins to shift his selling efforts to terminology, and the justification of value and price, you are close to paying top dollar for his car (retail) and taking bottom dollar for your trade (wholesale).

Watch the cash differences carefully when involved in terminology trading. If the salesman begins to hop around the contract by quoting you first retail to retail and then wholesale to wholesale, the cash differences should not change, unless the salesman is juggling figures.

Your best course of action is to forget terminology trading. If the salesman begins to sell by terminology, stop him as quickly as possible. Compute each car's value separately, and negotiate from those figures. Concentrate on narrowing the gap between what his car costs and what he will allow for your car in trade.

A very common used-car-deal ploy is splitting the profit. The salesman will tell you, very matter-of-factly, that he has only $300 profit in the car you want to buy. Now, he says, could anything be more fair than his offer to split his profit with you? How could you argue a better deal with him if he has already given you half of his profit? The catch is that you have no way of knowing exactly how much profit *is* in that particular used car. If he tells you his profit is only $300 and offers a discount of $150, it is quite possible he will make a profit of $550 provided his wholesale to retail spread is the usual $700. When confronted with "splitting the profit," ignore the figures and write your own deal according to your own computations.

BEFORE YOU SIGN

Before you sign on the dotted line, be certain that all condition-of-the-purchase replacement parts and/or repairs are spelled out in detail in the contract. Vague, ambiguous terminology could leave you no better off than if nothing at all had been written in the contract.

If it says, "Two new tires installed free of charge"—define "new" tires. Recaps or retreads will do the job as far as the salesman is concerned. Be certain the contract specifies "brand-new tires, not retreads."

If there is a cracked mirror (remote control), and the salesman writes, "Replace mirror at no charge to customer," spell out the type of mirror to be replaced. According to his written word, he could install a regular mirror instead of a remote control one.

"Oil change" does not mean "filter included." The salesman may replace just the oil and save the cost of the filter and one quart of oil.

"Check and inspect" does not mean replace and/or repair anything found wrong or defective. Add "Repair or replace if necessary" to the contract.

Suppose the engine runs rough. "Tune up engine" does not mean the car will receive new points, plugs, condensor, and a scope put on the engine to fine-tune it. The service department may only clean and reset the points and plugs, make minor adjustments on the carburetor and/or timing, and let it go at that. Specify parts replacement.

Used-Car Guideline

1. Acquire as much information as possible about the car in which you are interested before you make a commitment to pay a certain price and monthly payment, and finally, to buy it.
2. Do not be stubbornly silent, but do not give all your information away at once. Allow yourself enough room to move when discussing prices.
3. Do not express a solid, fixed interest in one car only, nor maintain an inflexible price, trade allowance, cash difference, or monthly payment.
4. Inspect the merchandise thoroughly; question the source of the merchandise; call the previous owner.
5. Question service—how good? and warranty—what does it include and for how long?
6. Write your own deal on any given car. Compute your own estimate of the value of your trade-in and the value of the car the salesman is selling.
7. Put everything in writing—leave no loose ends dangling.
8. Read everything word for word; double-check all figures.
9. Always determine beforehand just how much you can afford each month for a payment. (See chapter 12, "Financing.")
10. Realize that most strategies used throughout this book work while buying a used car—in decision making, handling the salesman, and negotiating.

11
Dealer Prep and Other Extras

ADD-ON CHARGES

DEALER PREPARATION. Commonly called dealer prep, dealer preparation is one of the fastest moneymakers in the business, for it is seldom questioned by the customer. It is justified by the dealer as a charge for services rendered, although often the only service performed is to wash the car. For this you may pay from $35 to $150. The dealer must convince you that you are indeed receiving something for your money, and that it is an indisputable charge. "All dealers charge it," you are told. "There are no exceptions and you must pay for the dealer prep. Your new car is inspected bumper-to-bumper by a mechanic prior to delivery." There is a factory checklist that the dealer is supposed to follow in prepping a car for delivery, for this the dealer is reimbursed by the factory. The checklist covers some fifty different areas of the car. Rather than follow the time-consuming checklist, most dealers choose to deliver the car and take their chances that problems will not develop. If problems do not develop, the dealer has been paid but has done nothing for the money. If a problem occurs that should have been caught and corrected by prep, the dealer corrects the problem and tells you that it is covered by the warranty; therefore, there is no charge to you.

There is no guaranteed method to tell whether or not dealer prep has been done. Even when dealer prep is done according to the checklist, problems can still develop. Your best defense is to personally check out the car prior to taking delivery and insist that any bugs found be remedied before you take it.

The charge for dealer prep is always in question. Should you pay for something not received, and should you pay for something already paid for by the factory? In any event, dealer prep, when paid, should never exceed 1 percent of the sticker price of the car you are buying.

Dealer prep may be buffered by the inclusion of one or more miscellaneous extras. The tack-on may read like this: "Dealer prep charge of $150 includes the preparation of this car for delivery, wash and wax, loaner car for warranty service work, first oil change and oil filter, first safety check or state inspection, first front end alighment, etc." This is designed to justify the charge, although if you totaled the real cost of these items, they would probably not exceed $50. In a situation such as this, your best move is to negotiate the dealer prep charge and tell the salesman that you are not interested in receiving an oil change or a free state inspection or a front end alignment, so he can just deduct the $150. You expect the car to be cleaned for delivery and for the factory recommended prep to be done, and you do not plan to pay for it.

Miscellaneous Charges. Handling charges, closing costs, and surcharges are another way of saying extra money for nothing. These charges are usually small in dollar amounts, but they do add up. A $10 handling charge on every car a dealer sells is an extra $1,000 in his pocket if he sells 100 cars in one month. These small charges are presented to you as being insignificant compared to the $6,500 you are spending for your car. As the salesman will point out, "Everybody pays it, and after all, it is only $10."

Ask the salesman exactly what you get for the $10, and if he cannot produce a tangible benefit for the money, do not buy the car until he removes the tack-on charge.

Never announce to the salesman that you do not plan to pay add-on charges until negotiations are completed and you have a signed management-approved deal. If you tell him early in the rounds of negotiating that you do not plan to pay, the salesman will simply hold back enough gross to cover the loss. He will then use the fact that he is not charging you the add-on to hold firm to his price, which will give him the negotiating advantage.

SERVICES RENDERED

Rustproofing. Rustproofing your new car is a paradox. The dealership is telling you that all the technological advances made by the factory mean nothing unless you have you car rustproofed, for it will fall apart within a few years without the rustproofing protection he offers. And maybe he is right.

What about the advertisements you see on television proclaiming deep dip, electrostatic priming, glasslike hardness of the painted surfaces, and so on? Unfortunately, these glorified word pictures do not carry a solid lifetime warranty that ensures problem-free rust protection. It is therefore advisable to have the work done if you plan to keep the car for any length of time, say in excess of 3 years. If you are a 1-to 3-year trader, you probably do not need the protection. There are five options available to you:

1. If the car was rustproofed by the dealer prior to its going into his inventory, the cost was added to the sticker price as a tack-on, and you pay for the service whether you want it or not, and whether you like it or not.
2. If it has not been done to the car, you can elect to pay the dealer for it.
3. Have it done by an outside, independent rustproofing service.
4. Do not have it done and take your chances with the elements.
5. Buy cans of pressure-spray material or a rustproofing kit and do it yourself.

The purpose of option one is to ensure a rustproof profit on every new car sold. Since the dealer is trying to force a profit, you should hold out for the deduction of the rustproofing cost and not buy unless and until it is removed. But save it for last. If the dealer knows this deduction is the only way you will buy, he will remove it.

Option two gives you free choice to take it or do without it. If you decide to have it done, it then becomes a negotiable item. Most dealers offer a bonus to their salesmen—usually $10 to $20—for selling a rustproofing to the customer. The dealer's cost for labor and material will be about $35, which brings his total investment to $55. For this service you are then charged from $80 to $150, depending on the dealer. To negotiate the rustproof cost, you must convince the salesman and his manager that the entire deal hinges on this one item. However, to succeed, you must also show the dealer a small profit on it. From there, negotiate upward in increments of $5 until you reach acceptance level. If the dealer refuses to negotiate the cost, tell him you will have it done elsewhere.

Option three is the elsewhere. Outside sources usually do a better job and offer a better guarantee than most dealerships who do rustproofing as a sideline.

Whether they are referred to as a guarantee or a warranty, read assurances carefully before you decide who will rustproof your new car. Beware the warranty that only repairs or replaces rust damage up to, but not over, the cost of the rustproofing, If rust problems develop during warranty coverage, you must pay for the excess cost over the rustproof cost.

The fourth option requires a decision: Will you get the use out of the investment for a rustproofing? If you do not plan to keep the car that long, don't have it done. The only benefit is higher resale value, but only if you sell it to a private owner. A dealer will not allow extra on trade value even though he may say he will.

The fifth option is one of convenience, economy, and personal motivation.

Some dealers offer a ScotchGard℠ service for new cars with cloth interiors. However, you can never be quite certain that the work was done because it is invisible to the eye once it dries on the material. Most automobile upholstery is stain resistant and will give you long life and ease of cleaning without your resorting to a spray-on costing extra money. Definitely refuse to pay for it if you encounter it as a tack-on item. Tell the dealer to prove it was done.

Dealer-Installed Equipment. This is a rip-off, plainly and simply put. With the exception of a vinyl top and other trim and dress-up items, anything installed by a dealer will not be as good as if it were done at the factory. Dealer-installed options are not covered by factory warranty and are usually cheap in design and quality.

If the car you have picked to buy does not have air-conditioning, do not even consider an add-on unit. If air is that important to you, shop until you find the car with factory-installed air-conditioning. If a salesman is desperate enough for a sale, he will tell you that his service department can install air-conditioning ''as good as if it came from the factory.'' Do not believe him. Add-on units almost always spell trouble to the buyer.

Radios, insignia floor mats, body side molding, mud flaps, sport or special chrome mirrors, special wheels and/or tires, and any other miscellaneous add-on items all cost more through a dealership for parts and labor for installation.

If you must have certain add-on equipment, shop department-store automobile centers or discount chain stores before you make final decisions. You may find lower prices and better service after the sale and installation of equipment. Some equipment can be installed by you for additional savings.

12
Financing

PAY CASH OR FINANCE?

IF YOU CAN AFFORD to pay cash and still have money in reserve, plan to pay for your purchase in cash. You may want to finance a small balance through the dealer, but only for the purpose of negotiating a better deal. You can always prepay the loan in a month or two. The prepayment penalty is usually nominal enough compared to the leverage it gives you when negotiating your deal.

When you must finance, choose a monthly payment that is comfortable for at least the next 12 months. The payment will be the same for the full term of the loan—usually 36 months—but your income will probably increase during your second and third years of ownership. If the monthly payment is affordable, buy the car. If you must stretch your budget to the point of collapse and sacrifice small luxuries, do not buy the car. Buy a less expensive car.

Never rely upon self-sacrifice to make a monthly payment affordable. It is easy to consider giving up smoking, drinking, or your one night out on the town each week to make up the deficit, but do not count on doing it when you really have to make the sacrifice. If your budget is so tight that you must forfeit part of your life style to buy the car, forfeit the car.

In most instances it is far better to know your limits, how much money you can borrow, and what it will cost you per month to repay it, before you take that first look at an automobile. If you do not know your limits you may waste a great deal of time shopping and haggling price and terms, only to discover that you can afford neither the down payment nor the monthly payment.

LENDING INSTITUTIONS

The Loan Officer. Never hesitate to deal directly with a lendor. The loan officer with whom you talk will not bite, will not look down his nose at you, and will try to avoid third-degree interrogation. He will ask no more questions than a dealer, will want no more credit information than a dealer, and will, for the most part, be more involved with the loan approval you need. Bear this in mind: The dealer cannot approve a loan, but the loan officer can.

Call for an appointment and explain that you plan to buy a new or used car. On the appointed day and hour, simply sit down and discuss the entire situation with the loan officer and fill out a credit application (*ap*). Ascertain exactly how much he will lend based on your income and outstanding bills. He can tell you how much you can borrow, a price range to maintain, the monthly payment, the rate of interest, the finance charge, and the cost of insurances and explain, in detail, your specific obligations in the matter, to include default, repossession, and recourse.

A loan officer can tell you exactly how much he will lend on a particular car with a given sticker price. Your down payment will be the difference between what the lendor will lend and the end-result deal you work with a dealer. You will need either X number of dollars (of your own or borrowed from another source), equity in your trade-in, or exceptionally strong credit (no down payment) to make your purchase.

Secondary Financing. Secondary financing generally means borrowing money from a source other than a bank. This money may be used for the full amount you need to buy a car or as a down payment to satisfy a bank's requirements. Most such loans are known as high-risk loans, which means the interest is usually higher, but the credit is more easily obtained. The major sources are finance companies, credit unions, and dealer financing.

Finance companies are called slaughterhouses in the trade. Their interest rates generally run from 15 percent to 23 percent, which is about double that of a bank or a credit union. If you need $500 to fill out a down payment for your new car, they are handy and easy and usually do not place a lien on your car. However, the installment contract you sign lets them pursue everything else you own if you default on the loan. Because of the exorbitant interest rates, use slaughterhouses only as a last resort, and read every word of everything you sign.

Credit unions vary in procedure, but their interest rates are comparable to those of a bank (11 percent to 12 percent). Credit unions offer ease of payment (automatic payroll deduction each week) and are more lenient on credit requirements and approval. They may be used for full or partial financing on your purchase. Caution: most credit unions freeze any savings you might have at the time they grant a loan. If you have $500 accumulated, you may not be able to touch it until the loan is paid off. It is best to transfer your accumulated funds to an outside savings account before you make application to a credit union, if you feel you might need the funds.

There are two types of dealer "paper": that which is written and turned over to a bank (the bank controls the credit and terms), and that which the dealer backs himself—he grants the credit, sets the terms, takes the payments, and takes the car if you do not pay. Dealer-backed financing is usually found on used-car dirt lots and offers little or no money down, easy terms, high interest rates, and quick repossession when you get behind in payments. Generally, the down payment will be about what the dealer has invested in a car—if the price is $500 and he got the car for $100, your down payment will be the $100. Immediately he recaptures his investment, and any payments you make, plus the interest charged, is his profit. If he must repossess the car he keeps all money received and sells the car again. He may sell the same car five times, make a $500 profit, and still have the car on his lot for sale. Avoid this situation. Go to a bank, credit union, or even a slaughterhouse first.

If you have had credit problems or rejections, are a slow payer, or have filed for bankruptcy, tell the person with whom you are dealing; never try to hide anything. Silence about past problems will speak against you when the truth is discovered; your honesty will definitely speak to your benefit. Everything you have ever done with regard to credit is on file somewhere, waiting for a phone call to release the information. Even your application for credit is noted in your credit file. If you have been rejected by several lendors, it will show on a routine credit run and may cause an automatic rejection by the investigating lendor; if others have already rejected you there must be a reason.

When you apply for dealership financing, the information is called in to a lending institution (usually a bank) for credit approval. The lendor has only this phone call and the information he is given to make a loan decision. The lendor has not had a chance to meet you and does not know you. Your personal visit could make the difference between loan approval and rejection if your credit is the least bit shaky. However, some lendors will encourage you to go through the dealer, mostly because a repossession will fall upon the shoulders of the dealer if it is written on dealer paper. If a bank does not want to deal with you personally, shop around a bit. Make a few phone calls to compare interest rates and charges. A 1 percent lower rate on $5000 will save about $150 on a 3-year loan.

Used-Car Financing. All the above financing sources will consider a used-car loan. However, the interest rates are progressively higher and the duration of loan progressively lower according to the car's age. On a used-car loan you must really shop rates and terms to save money because of the wide variance among lendors.

FINANCE INSURANCES

There are three basic types of insurance that can be written into an installment contract: credit life (CL), accident & health (A&H), and comprehensive (comp). In some instances liability insurance can also be included, but CL, A&H, and comp are the most frequently used by lendors and dealers. All three forms can be included in one monthly payment.

Credit life insurance is basically decreasing term insurance. It will pay off the balance owing on your loan if you die. The amount of coverage decreases as you pay down the balance of the loan and has nothing to do with the car's market value when you die. If you double up or triple up on payments, thus reducing the balance of your loan, it will not pay what your balance should have been had you not doubled up on payments. If you prepay the entire loan you will receive a rebate on the cost of any insurances—just as you would on the finance charges—and the coverage stops. If you already have more life insurance than you really need, skip the credit life.

Accident and health insurance is geared to your monthly payment. It becomes active and makes your monthly payment for you when your normal income stops because of illness, accident, or disability. It does not reflect upon your credit standing since you will not miss a payment if you are off work for a few months. *Note:* You must file for the benefits before the payments will be made for you. If the dealer does not have forms, the lendor who holds your note can mail you one. Once you have filed, the payments are made automatically for as long as you are sick or disabled. If you return to work and then are off again, a new claim form must be filed to reactivate the coverage. The customary waiting period before the coverage begins to pay varies from company to company. It is usually 10 days retroactive to the first day you miss work. A&H does not cover strikes, layoffs, being fired, and the like. A&H is nonconflicting insurance and will pay benefits regardless of other health insurance you may have in effect.

Because A&H is more popular than CL, dealers do their best to discourage you from taking it alone—they lose the higher profit on CL. If you want the A&H badly enough, you will take the CL because you will be led to believe that they must be bought as a package. This is not true. Each is an individual protection and can be included in your monthly payment as such. If you want only the A&H, insist upon A&H and tell the dealer, "If I cannot have the A&H alone, forget about the financing altogether. I will get my own money." The dealer will not chance losing the finance charge profit (about 20 percent of the total finance charge) for the sake of holding out for the CL profit.

Comprehensive insurance is generally required by the lendor to protect his investment. If you have a healthy balance on the car and it is smashed up, someone must pick up the pieces, and the lendor does not want it to be him. You have the choice of getting your own coverage or taking a plan through the lendor right along with the other insurances. The advantage to taking it through the lendor is that the rate is usually lower and it is easier than shopping for your own plan. If you have had a few accidents and find it difficult to get your own comprehensive insurance, take the comp offered by the lendor/dealer.

DEALERSHIP FINANCING TACTICS

A dealer sells financing just as he sells a car. Each dealer you encounter is, in essence, his own lending institution and can offer the advantages of one-stop shopping. Financing represents a profit to the dealer, even though the paperwork will be carried on the books of a local lending institution, and you will make your payments to that same lendor. The lendor also handles all facets of pursuing and collecting delinquent accounts. Most dealers work with more than one lendor.

Because of competition, a basic greed for the dollar, and the realization that they were losing the finance profit on three of every four cars they sold, dealers have moved toward using the services of a business manager in ever-increasing numbers each year. The major function of a business manager is to sell financing, on dealer paper, to all customers making a car purchase at the dealership. However, he also advises the dealership on investments, floor planning, and any other incidentals regarding the financial structure of the business. He sells financing with the same enthusiasm the salesman used to sell you your car.

The business manager can work for you or against you depending upon your individual financing plans. If you want to pay cash or finance through your credit union (his biggest competitor for your finance dollar), he will do his best to change your thinking. When he enters the closing room at the request of your salesman, his entire plan is to switch you over to his side and finance through his dealership. If you plan to finance through another source, maintain your position throughout his presentation. If you have no plans, or if your credit rating is the least bit shaky, listen to what he has to say; he may be able to help you. Business managers are well trained in credit requisites, down payments, and alternate finance sources, and most managers have at least one or two favors coming from lendors on borderline cases.

Then there is the other side of the business manager, if you are one of those who plans outside financing. His ploys include misquotes, shuffling of quotes, and overt misrepresentation. He may quote you a higher monthly payment than should be and then say, "Here is where I can save you some money. Instead of $130 a month, I can write the paper on this for $126.50, which will save you $100 over the length of the loan." In reality, the payment should have been $126.50 from the start.

Another method: The business manager can show you in black and white in his time-loan tables that the balance you need to finance will cost you $130 a month. He will then show—in the same set of tables—that $126.50 will save you $100, and he will write the finance papers for $126.50. The evidence is right up front in black and white; however, the $126.50 is without the accident and health and credit life insurances. Your savings is not based on a $100-better deal or interest rate, but rather on deletion of the insurances; the balance due and the finance charges remain the same throughout.

The business manager may intentionally misquote a monthly payment and show you a savings in black and white. But this time it is overt misrepresentation. For this to be successful, you must sign a blank or incompletely filled-in finance contract. The business manager must then see to it that you do not receive a copy of the contract. Since it is blank, but signed, he can fill in whatever figures he desires and ship it off to the lendor to collect the dealer's money.

When you receive your payment book from the lendor and discover the higher monthly payment, you will be given variations of three basic stories by the business manager. He will pacify you and swear that it was nothing more than a simple misunderstanding.

1. You may be told that the lower figure originally quoted did not

include the insurances (CL and A&H). It was assumed that you wanted them since you signed the insurance blocks on the contract. Inclusion of the insurances automatically raised the monthly payment.

Alternate: The lower figure quoted did not include the sales tax. It was assumed that you would be paying it separately, direct to the state. Inclusion of the tax automatically raised the monthly payment.

2. If a trade-in is involved that has a balance due on it, he will tell you that the payoff on your existing loan was higher than expected, which automatically raised the monthly payment.

3. If a story does not fit the situation, the business manager will flatly deny that he quoted you the lower figure and insist that the payment you received from the lendor is the same as quoted from the beginning. It is a simple matter of your memory and your word against his. If you made note of the payment quoted, he will tell you that it is too late now since the paperwork has already been processed through the lendor.

Your best defense is to never, never sign anything that contains blank spaces or incomplete information. Whether the influence to sign a blank contract stems from your pride, ego, or salesman and business manager insistence, be certain there are no loose ends attached to the deal you sign. If you are told that a particular space does not apply to your particular purchase, insert "N/A" (not applicable) in the space.

If you do not understand what you are reading or signing, have it explained to you. You have the right to know exactly what everything means within the body of the contract or agreement to purchase. If you sign without understanding and a problem arises, you cannot plead ignorance as your recourse. However, if you sign a blank contract at the insistence of a salesman or manager, you have recourse if he misrepresents verbally and fills in a blank space contrary to agreement.

You have the right to receive a copy of everything you sign, at the time you sign it, not a day later. If you are told that someone who is not immediately available must fill in the blanks, tell him that you will not sign until the blanks are filled in. If it means returning the following day to sign, do it. Any sales manager worth his salt can fill in the necessary information on an installment contract if he has a time-payment book. Whatever the reason given, do not sign blank.

If you are victimized by an unfair contract, your first move is to call the dealership and make the dealer aware of the discrepancy. Tell him that you expect it to be corrected, ignore the excuse for why it happened, and obtain his promise that everything will be handled properly. Then call the lending institution handling the loan and make the installment loan officer aware of the situation. Never tell the dealer that you plan to call the lendor; let him dig his own grave. If he contacts the lendor as promised, all the better for you. If the lendor is aware of a problem and hears nothing from the dealer, it will speak against him. If you receive no satisfaction, call or write the Federal Trade Commission. (See chapter 14, "External Recourse.")

REPOSSESSION

Repossession (repo) need not be a dirty word, nor does it always mean that you lose everything you have put into your car prior to the repo. If you are familiar with a few rules and procedures, it can, at times, work to your benefit.

The two basic forms of repossession are voluntary and aggressive.

Voluntary repo: You realize that you can no longer continue to maintain your monthly payments and, of your own free will, you turn the car over to the dealer or lendor holding the note on it.

Aggressive repo: You are in default of your note or loan and the lendor or the dealer sends someone to collect the car, whether you like it or not.

Of the two, voluntary repo does the least damage to your credit standing. Nobody had to chase you and track you down to get the car. You were responsible enough to realize that you could no longer afford to make payments, and you turned the car in without pressure from the lendor. It is critical that you make the first move and turn the car in. The determining factor of the two repo's is, did you take it back or was it taken?

When you realize that you cannot maintain the payments, call the lendor to see whether something cannot be worked out to make him happy. Usually a lendor will defer a payment or accept an interest-only payment to help you keep the car and get back on your feet. He may also rewrite the loan to give you even more time. But again, you must make the first move.

Deferred payment means that you make no payment for that particular month and pick up your normal payments beginning the following month. You compensate for the deferred month at the end of your loan term.

Interest-only payment means that you pay only the interest portion of your regular monthly payment. This will always be a variable amount, for the total interest due in any given month decreases as the loan becomes older. This gives the lendor his profit on the loan and makes it easier for you to maintain continuity of pay history.

A lendor will usually try for an interest payment first, and if that is impossible he will offer deferred payment. Most lendors will grant a deferred payment or interest-only payment once each year for the life of the loan. If you have already used either the deferred or interest-only solution in a given year, he may suggest, or you may request, a rewrite on the loan.

A rewrite means cancelling the existing loan and writing a fresh loan. This requires a fresh application with a new credit check and credit approval or rejection. A rewrite really depends upon your credit rating, your past payment history, and how the lendor feels about starting all over again.

You will lose a little more money on a rewrite, for you are starting a new loan with fresh interest, but if you can choose between rewriting the loan and turning the car in, take the rewrite. If you back them up, and if the lendor is willing to make two consecutive concessions, you can obtain 75 days between payments—30 for a deferred payment, 45 for a rewrite.

If you have used these options and still find yourself on the verge of a repo, try to sell the car yourself for more than you owe on it. If you sell it, even for break-even money, your credit record is pure and clean, and neither form of repo will show on a future credit check. All that will show is that you prepaid the loan, which is a good reflection on your credit record.

Get a closeout or payoff figure from your lendor, compute a selling price for your car, run an advertisement, and hope for the best. Never, never let a prospective buyer know why you are selling your car. Tell him that you plan to buy a new car and want no trade-in or that you have one too many cars in your family, but never say that you are forced to sell because of financial reasons.

A buyer can assume your loan balance, take over your monthly payments, and pay you the difference between the selling price and the balance due. A loan assumption is subject to lendor approval, and your buyer's credit must be at least as good as your credit, if not better. The major advantage to the buyer is that he saves the large chunk of interest paid at the beginning of a loan's life. Before you run your ad, see whether your lendor will take an assumption.

If you cannot sell your car or find someone to assume your loan, do not play hide-and-seek with the lendor. When you have taken all action possible and still find your back to the wall, turn the car in. If *they* come to *you*, your credit will show a black mark—aggressive repossession.

Once your car goes back to the lendor, you are still not out of the woods. The car must be sold, and you have the first right to purchase (redemption) and save the blemish on your credit. If you do not buy it and it is sold for less than your balance due, you will owe a deficit balance—the difference between what you owed and what the car sold for. If the deficit balance is ridiculously high—the wholesale valuation was $1,800, you owed $1,800, and the car was sold for $1,000—you can appeal the deficit balance. Appeal usually requires legal assistance or arbitration and can be time-consuming and expensive. But it is better to pay several hundred in legal fees than to be stuck with an unfair $800 debt with nothing to show for it. If you are financially destitute, seek help from your local Legal Aid Society.

CAR FINANCING GUIDELINE

Whether you are dealing with a dealership business manager or a lendor, there are certain questions you should ask regarding your loan.

1. What is the annual percentage rate (APR)? Most dealers (and some lendors) will quote an add-on rate of interest that is not the true, simple-interest rate. Six percent add-on is about 11.04 percent, depending on loan duration. There is about 1 percent that can be given away at the discretion of the dealer or lendor to reduce your APR. Shop for the best rate.
2. What is the amount of the loan; total balance due or borrowed?
3. What is the dollar cost of the finance charges and insurances?
4. What is the length of the loan (term or duration in months)?
5. What is the monthly payment? When are the first and last payments due and how much is each?
6. How much is the prepayment penalty; how is it computed?
7. How much are the closing costs and/or any other miscellaneous costs?
8. What is the grace period (time before the loan becomes in default)?
9. What is the charge for a late payment? When is a payment considered late?

DELIVERY

When all the contracts have been signed and approved and the money—whether cash or financed dollars—changes hands, it is time to take delivery of your car. Do not take delivery unless and until all contingencies have been resolved to your complete satisfaction. If the car is missing equipment or still has a malfunction that was to have been corrected, you do not have to take the car. If you desire, you can cancel the deal for breach by nonperformance. Once you take the car, the dealer can take his time satisfying his obligations—the old stall routine. Nothing will make a dealer or salesman move faster than the words: "It does not have what you agreed to furnish. I do not want the car like this. I won't take it." At this point he will either fix it while you wait, ask you to come back for the car a little later in the day, or try to talk you into taking the car on the promise that the work will be done.

This is when it takes tremendous will power to bite the bullet and refuse delivery. If you give in now you may continue to give in until you eventually just quit trying.

When you discover problems that were not remedied or equipment that is missing, make a big deal out of it. To obtain anything from a dealer, you must convince him that it is extremely important to you and that you absolutely will not take the car unless the problem is fixed. The more insistent the salesman is that you take the car, the more you should question his motives. Ask him, "Why is it so important to you that I take the car now? Why are you trying to push me into taking the car? Are you hiding something or is it that you do not plan to fix the car when I bring it back?"

Treat your new car to a used-car inspection—go over every square inch and check out everything that pushes, pulls, or switches on and off. Assume nothing. Everything corrected now is that much less for the future.

All this puts the salesman on the defensive, and his immediate reaction will be to agree with everything you say and begin to expedite solutions. At this point he knows he is very close to losing the sale and the commission he worked so hard to get. If, however, he insists that you take the car, expect the very worst when you return for corrections and promised work.

Most times you will find that dealers take care of the large items and tend to overlook the small items. The logic is that you will create problems for the dealership on a large item but will eventually forget about a small item. If you have something coming, collect it, no matter how small.

13
Service Department

THE WARRANTY

MOST PEOPLE THINK that a 12-month, 12,000-mile new-car warranty covers 100 percent of everything on the car for the full 12 and 12. However, most warranties have a 90-day clause that covers everything for 90 days and covers only critical, mechanical drive-train components for the balance of the warranty. What is covered and for how long varies among manufacturers. Some will not cover electrical parts and squeaks and rattles after 90 days. Some offer a fixed time limit and extended mileage—12 months and 50,000 miles, whichever occurs first. Because there are so many different warranties, have the the salesman explain, in detail, exactly what is covered and when, what is not covered, the required maintenance to keep the warranty in effect, and the maintenance cost. And then read the warranty word for word. Question anything you do not understand.

There are, in some instances, items that are covered but are not advertised as being part of the warranty. For example, the factory may be willing to pay for a front-end alignment or may extend warranty benefits on certain items after warranty expiration. Service managers are aware of these secret warranty items but do not normally hand out the information willingly. When in doubt about something amiss, contact the Federal Trade Commission.

Sale of Extended Warranty Coverage. Most dealers offer an extended warranty you can buy at extra cost. This is really a service contract similar in nature to those sold on major appliances. It does not matter who makes the profit on a service contract—the dealer or the factory or an outside independent. The important question is, do you really need it, and do you really want it.

A service contract generally covers only critical drive-train components and internal engine problems. It is safe to presume that any serious original-manufacture defects in your drive-train are going to develop within the normal warranty 12 and 12 coverage and will be paid for by the factory. It is further safe to presume that if nothing goes seriously wrong in the first 12 and 12, the car will make it at least another 24 months and 24,000 miles, provided you perform prescribed maintenance on schedule and do not abuse the car. The odds of something serious happening between 12 and 12 and 36 and 36 are so slight that it is hardly worth spending several hundred dollars for protection you probably won't use. You can replace a lot of surface equipment for several hundred dollars—alternator, power steering unit, master brake cylinder—things you would have to pay for anyway if you bought the service contract. Money on top of money.

Consider saving the initial investment for a service contract and creating your own warranty repair fund, unless:

1. You plan to keep the car longer than 3 years.
2. You put exceptionally high mileage on a car and will exceed 36,000 to 40,000 miles in 3 years. (Some contracts have a mileage restriction; others do not.)
3. You are notorious for destroying engines and transmissions.

Read the offered service contract word for word and ask these questions:

1. Exactly what is covered for how long and how many miles?
2. Who does the work, and what happens if they are unavailable or cannot fix it?
3. Is the contract renewable upon expiration and what is the cost for renewal?
4. Is there a limit on occurrences and must you pay a deductible each time your car needs work? (Limits and deductibles are no bargain.)
5. Must you continue to pay the high cost of dealership maintenance items—oil changes, filters—or can you do your own?

Factory-Backed Extended Warranty. Be wary of factory-sponsored extended warranties. The main intention of the factory in offering such a warranty is to stimulate sales. Another reason is to push a car that is not selling because of a known defect. In the mid-1970s, a certain compact had a tendency to overheat and lock up the engine. When sales began to drop, the manufacturer, in an effort to diminish public fears of buying, placed a 5-year, 60,000-mile warranty on the car. That may sound good on paper, but what if you are stuck in the middle of nowhere with a car that will not move 1 inch under its own power? If a particular car has a reputation for failing under certain conditions, the extended warranty means literally nothing compared to the headaches that can be created. Do not be lulled into any sense of false security offered by this type of extended warranty. If your instinct says don't buy, then don't buy. Once they have your money, it is a long road back to break even when problems begin to develop.

HANDLING SERVICE PROBLEMS

First, before you become frustrated to the point of tears, find out exactly what is wrong with your car. This requires a visit to the service department. If it is something simple and easily fixed, you will have wasted a lot of time, grief, and anxiety for nothing. Realize that a recurring problem may be caused by more than one part or a cluster of parts. A steering problem may be caused by one of a hundred or more small component parts. It is important to know exactly what was done and what part was bad each time you take your car in.

Be aware that it is not the fault of the service department if you need your car in 1 hour and you don't get it—unless it was promised, and it is not the department's fault if a particular part is not in stock on the very day your car needs it. Realize that dealing with a service department requires a little diplomacy, some politics, and a patient attitude. It never hurts to be polite and considerate. When you run into a grumpy service manager, give him a big smile—win him over.

Reduce It to Writing. Service personnel are always, and notoriously, short of time. You will save their time and your own if your problems are neatly spelled out in black and white. There are three reasons why it is important to keep a copy of your complaint list:

1. It gives you something to double-check against when you retrieve your car.
2. It helps you maintain a running record of your visits to the service department and may itself become the permanent record of your visits.
3. It represents tangible evidence that you can produce when confronting either dealership management or the factory representative.

Bear in mind that several different people may be working on your car—mechanics, bodymen—throughout the day. For mutual convenience, categorize that which you want done. Put all mechanical work in one section and all body work together as best as possible. Categorizing tells the service manager in an instant what needs to be done by whom, so that when you ask, "Can you do all this today?" he can give you a reasonably accurate answer.

Appointments. For best results and cooperation it is always best to make a firm appointment prior to your visit to the service department. Even if you think it is a take-a-quick-look-at-it visit, an appointment is advisable. Before you leave, here are a few dos and don'ts to observe:

1. Set your appointment and *be on time*.
2. Briefly review your list of complaints with the service manager. Explain what your car does and when it does it.
3. Never tell a service manager that he can keep your car for a few days or for as long as it takes to get it done. This is an automatic put-it-off-til-tomorrow clue to do cars with get-it-done-today status.
4. When you arrive for your car and the manager tells you that they could not get it done, immediately schedule another appointment. "Something came up and I don't need the car after all. Can you finish it tomorrow? When can you?"
5. Each time you are unhappy with the service performed on your car, let your salesman know as soon as possible. The first time, tell your salesman only. The second and third times, tell your salesman and his sales manager. The fourth time, tell both of them and the general manager and/or dealership owner. The fifth time, it is time to talk to the factory representative and start writing letters.
6. Whenever possible, have all parties concerned present when complaining. If the service manager defends his position, it is to your advantage to know just what he has to say.

Records. Now is the time to document the visit, to inscribe a permanent record of the situation while everything is fresh in your mind. Your memory is not infallible and the chance of something being forgotten is very high.

Any service department can have a complete record pulled in a few moments that will show everything that was ever done to your car—cost, time, labor, parts, and who did the work. During a dispute, you should be as well prepared to defend your position with names, dates, and items.

A simple but effective system is a small file box that contains index cards. It is easy to use and maintain. There is no need for an elaborate numerical, alphabetical, or cross-indexed system to ensure the best results. Just be faithful to your system and be consistent. It does little good to keep half of any information if you ever plan to use any of it.

Every contact with the dealership should be noted on a card with the date, the names of person(s) talked to or involved, the nature of the problem, what was done and how long it took, the name of the mechanic, the final disposition, and whether or not you were satisfied. Add significant comments as necessary; details help. If you are not certain of terminology, ask questions. "Worked on the brakes" can cover anything from the master cylinder to the caliper clips to a simple adjustment. Specifically what was done? Vague answers will produce vague records. "We fixed the squeak" is not good enough. What was the source of the problem? Always note the car's mileage on your records, both when you dropped it off and when you picked it up. Excessive mileage—more than 5 to 10 miles—means they used your car and your fuel for errands. Expect 1 to 4 miles on the car for road testing; complain about an excess.

Even though you may be receiving beautiful service, maintain records from your very first visit. In most dealerships, the service department gives extra-effort, super-duper service to all fresh customers. This is a staged, lulling tactic designed to make you think that their service is fantastic. After the image is cast and the impression stamped upon your mind, the lullaby stops—not abruptly, but more as a tapering-off of the extra effort. When things start going sour, you lose fighting power if you do not have complete and accurate records. Also, just because something was fixed does not mean it was fixed permanently. If you must eventually go to court, you will need evidence.

HANDLING POOR SERVICE

When you are getting nowhere with your service manager or he tells you that nothing can be done with your car, what then? You can argue with him until you turn blue or until he walks away from you. You can find your salesman and drop your problems in his lap. You can walk away from the situation, firm in the belief that to complain further is futile, and vow never to buy another car from them. Or, you can find out exactly whom you must see and with whom you must talk to obtain results.

At this point you are concerned only with the name of the person who can say, "Fix it and do it right." As long as lower-echelon personnel can solve your problems you need go no higher, but when the lower ranks cease and desist, it is time to appeal to a higher power. When you find out who he is, sit down and lay out your problems. This means that you will need the records you have been faithfully keeping. It also means that you should be prepared to handle the "All-American Runaround."

The All-American Runaround is a pacifier given to a customer to quiet his anger, and it usually boils down to a series of delaying tactics. If, for example, the general manager of the dealership is the only person who can say "Fix it" and if, after listening to your complaint, he does say "Fix it," you may be on your way to resolving your problems. Then again, he may say "Fix it" just to get you off his back. As soon as you leave he may call the service manager and tell him to start delaying tactics.

At some point you will realize you are being put off. Upset, you will return to the general manager, and he will proceed to become upset right along with you. He will assure you that the party responsible for your problems will suffer severely. He may even fake a blasting phone call to the service manager or he may simply promise that everything is just a misunderstanding and will be taken care of, and of course, you have his deepest apologies. You return to the service department, confident that your car will finally be fixed, and again the delaying tactics begin. You may be confronted with a different set of excuses, but the principle and the end result remain the same: Your car is not fixed. By now you are ready either to throw in the towel or to make one last effort to give them a chance to do the right thing. And suppose you do and suppose they don't? What then?

To begin, you must be able to recognize a delaying tactic. A delaying tactic is designed for one purpose: to buy time. If enough time passes, you will either give up the effort or become docile enough to do it their way. If their way means splitting the bill, you will split the bill rather than continue to fight. Anything that consumes time can be considered a delaying tactic. Here are a few of the most common:

1. "Our backlog of scheduled work is 10 days. Call us then."
2. "The mechanic who normally handles that specific problem is in the hospital (is home sick, just quit, is booked solid for the next 2 weeks)."
3. "Bring your car in tomorrow and leave it." (When you return for your car you will be told that they could not get to it and to bring it back tomorrow. This can happen until you tire of bringing your car in and leaving it.)
4. "We will have to order a special part to make the repair." (This is a good one.)
5. "The factory representative will have to look at this before we make

the repair. We will call you on the day that he is to be here.'' (Don't hold your breath waiting for the call).

When you recognize a delaying tactic, you must go back to the salesman or sales manager for another session. And the sooner the better.

The Attack. ''Mr. General Manager, your service manager just told me that he cannot schedule my car to be fixed for 2 weeks.''

''Gee, Mr. Customer, that is too bad, but there is nothing I can do about the work load they have. You know, there are other people who have problems also, and if they are first in line I guess you will just have to wait. But I am certain that this will be handled properly just as soon as they can get to your car. In fact, I will call the service manager and tell him to call you immediately if he has a cancellation of an appointment. How does that sound?''

''Mr. General Manager, that sounds terrific, but what about the fact that this is my fourth time in for the same problem? That would really put me first in line, would it not? I think that your service manager can do a better job of scheduling his work than to offer me a 2-week delay, don't you agree? Why don't you give him a call and see whether he can do it sooner, and I will not have to bother you anymore with this.'' (This implies that you will continue coming to him until your problem is solved.) ''Better yet, let's go to the service department together and see if we can't resolve this problem by putting our heads together.

''Mr. General Manager, your service manager just told me that the mechanic who normally handles this type of problem will not be available for some time. You did tell me that this would be handled, and I really believe that it will. To save us both a lot of time and trouble I would like you to call XYZ Garage and authorize them to do the work and let them know they can bill your dealership for the cost.''

The general manager will raise stiff objections to this suggestion: ''We cannot do that. Just be patient and we will fix your car for you.''

To which you reply: ''I do not doubt that at all. But I do not plan to wait 6 months until it is done. If your service department cannot handle the problem, you will have to farm the work out to another garage and pay for it, cash out of pocket.'' *Note:* You can have the work done by another source, but most times a dealership will refuse to pay and you will end up in a small claims court to collect. Good records will help you win your case.

When you are presented with a parts delay, find out exactly what parts are necessary to fix your car and jot down the name of each individual part, complete with the part number when possible. Some dealers will give you a parts slip or a receipt to confirm the fact that the part was indeed ordered. Get an approximate arrival time. If the part is coming from a zone warehouse it should be a matter of a few days. A factory-ordered part could take several weeks, and import parts several months. When the time comes and goes without word of your part's arriving, call to confirm whether it is in or not. If it is not, begin to look for the part needed at other dealers' parts departments or at parts supply outlets. When you have found the parts needed, go to the dealership and give them a chance to quit making excuses and perform. Simply say, "I have found the parts that you say are holding up the work on my car. I am going to give you until (say, 2 days from now) to secure the parts from your own sources, and if you cannot, I want you to buy those parts from my source and fix my car." Or, "Since there will be no problem securing the necessary parts, I would like to schedule my car in for the work to be done." If the dealer cannot—or will not—do so, make a call to someone higher up and lay it on the line.

Here, there are several elements to consider: Are you receiving valid reasons why they cannot fix your car, or excuses? There are few legitimate reasons that cannot be worked out provided the dealer is willing to co-operate and makes a decent effort to satisfy your complaint. Remember that when a service complaint has gone far enough to warrant a visit to the general manager, it has gone far enough so that the dealership may not really plan to fix your car. Therefore, treat all reasons as excuses until proven otherwise. You will hear a lot of excuses from the general manager. His main goal is to get you off his back. Your goal is to get your car fixed. Be prepared to hunt him down, outwait him, and, if necessary, raise a little hell. He will promise anything to get you to leave him alone. But you want results, not promises. Be persistent.

The general manager is playing the numbers. He knows that he will lose X number of customers throughout any given year, for whatever reason, but he also knows that he will pick up X number of customers from his competition for the same reasons he lost his. If the general manager has this attitude, avoids you, and does not seem to want to satisfy your complaints, it is time to see the factory representative.

The Factory Representative. In a dispute between the customer and the dealership regarding warranty work, the factory representative (rep) is just about the final word on whether the work is covered and whether the factory will pay. The rep can also arbitrate seemingly hopeless mechanical problems (perhaps a cash adjustment) and authorize out-of-warranty work or work not normally covered—that is, when you can talk to him. He can be more elusive than a general manager, because the rep floats from dealer to dealer and not necessarily on a set schedule. If your dealer is derelict in advising you when the factory rep will be at his dealership to handle complaints, call or write the zone office nearest you to set an appointment. It may even be possible to resolve your problem over the phone.

The factory rep is not someone you can butter up, sway easily, or otherwise sneak one past. He is trained to listen patiently to your problems, never to become rattled, and to save the factory money. Every time he says *no*, the factory saves money. Every time he says *yes*, it is only because he must. He knows exactly what is covered and what is not at any given time in the warranty life, what secret warranties are in effect and apply to your case, and exactly how to handle the borderline, reasonable-doubt cases. A reasonable-doubt case could be a question of time; the warranty on the problem expired 2 weeks ago but you insist that you have had the problem since the day you bought the car. He must decide whether to accept your word and give you the claim, argue it out, reason it out, or tell you *no*. If it is a borderline case, he will try to dissuade you from pursuing the issue and convince you to give up the fight. Again, if he can convince you not to push the issue, the factory saves money. If he feels that you really plan to pursue it aggressively, he may decide to yield to your persistence. If he can say *no* and maintain your good will as a customer, he will do so.

How does he know he can say *no* and get away with it? Mostly by the way you present your story to him. A display of confidence weakens his position. Act as if you do not doubt your position and as if you firmly believe that the work should be done by the dealer and paid for by the factory. If you approach him meekly and are hesitant to ask for what may rightly be yours, he will take advantage of you. Be calm, but be firm.

Do not use words such as: "Could you" or "Would you" to ask for a remedy to your problems. This is a negative, closed-end question that expresses doubt and makes it too easy for him to say, "No, I cannot." Use instead words such as: "When can you? When can the service department fix this?"

Do not use your salesman as a runner. The rep can tell him anything and later deny it. He can also say *no* more easily to the salesman than to an irate customer. If you have taken the time to work things out and have been unsuccessful, it is time to seek external recourse. But before you do, tell the top man with whom you have been talking what you plan to do and give him one last chance to produce results. Do not threaten or tip your hand until you get a firm *no*, and if you get a firm *no*, give him the worst you can put together.

GUIDELINE FOR COMPLAINING

1. Try to resolve your service problems at the service-department level.
2. When you receive no satisfaction at that level, go to your salesman, then to the sales manager, then to the general manager or owner of the dealership.
3. Present your case with supportive evidence (records), and keep it brief and to the point. Get the general manager to agree with you that you do have a valid complaint. Let him know exactly what you expect him to do about your complaint, what will make you happy, and when you expect it done.
4. Never threaten unless you are prepared to take immediate action. If you threaten legal action, the general manager may call your bluff and tell you to sue him.
5. Be prepared to continue to return to the general manager with your complaint until it is satisfied. Put a time limit on his commitment—"How soon?" Have him put any past broken promises in writing and sign them. Each time you must see him, go through your entire complaint, start to finish—wear him out by talking.

14
External Recourse

DOES IT DO ANY GOOD?

EXTERNAL RECOURSE for the consumer is sometimes difficult to obtain. The agencies are there, the addresses are available, the people exist to whom you can talk, but by the time most people pursue a recourse it is too late to really achieve any reasonable form of satisfaction. At best, your complaint registered with the proper agencies can help protect someone else.

The best recourse available to you is preventive. Simply put, check everything out before you buy. If you have done all that and you have still encountered a problem, an avenue of release is needed to alleviate the frustrations you are experiencing—and to resolve the problem when and if possible.

Consumer protection and action agencies and groups are not always the panacea to your problems. They do not—and cannot—guarantee results, and relieving the burden of the problem from your mind may be the only satisfaction you receive. It may be necessary to resort to legal measures or militant tactics to get the satisfaction you want and deserve. For simple matters of irritation when you want to tell someone but do not want to become involved in a court battle, the following agencies are at hand to assist you.

AGENCIES

Better Business Bureau (BBB). The BBB is your best prepurchase preventive medicine. This Bureau will give you, for the most part, basic information about which businesses are legitimate and which you may want to avoid. It can usually give you a history of the business, who's who in the business, and, most important to you, how many complaints have been registered against the company by dissatisfied customers.

The BBB works only if people use it. Those who have already suffered problems with a business need to report them to the BBB so that those who have not yet bought have something to investigate. When a complaint has been filed, the business in question naturally has the right to defend its position, so there is a balance to the system all the way around.

If there is no BBB in your town and you must make a toll call to a nearby town to register a complaint or investigate a company, do it. It may cost a few cents for the call, but it will be worth the investment.

The BBB is also involved in arbitration settlements between the consumer and the business. However, the business has the option not to participate. Both parties agree before hand to abide by the decision of BBB. The abitrator then hears both sides of the story and makes the decision. (Records help.)

Consumer Protection Agencies. Similar in effectiveness to the Better Business Bureau, the consumer protection agencies are more concerned with consumer safety than poor business practices, although they do become involved. They will act as mediator between consumer and business in areas of financial loss and customer dissatisfaction, but their primary concern is protection before the fact, not mediation after the fact. Consumer protection agencies are found at local, county, and state levels. Check your phone book.

Federal Trade Commission (FTC), Washington, D.C. 20580. The primary concern of the FTC is fair trade practices. Although it does not handle individual cases, the FTC can be a great source of consumer information on warranties, installment contracts, and guidelines and is a complaint-lodging medium though no assurance of individual follow-up can be given.

National Highway Traffic Safety Administration (NHTSA), 400 Seventh Street, SW, Washington, D.C. 20590. The primary concern of NHTSA is new-car safety-related items. If your problem is a safety-related item, you can call a toll-free number to report it: 800-424-9393 (in Washington D.C., call 426-0123), or write.

National Advertising Review Board (NARB), 845 Third Avenue,

New York, N.Y. 10022. The concern of the NARB is for truth and accuracy in advertising. If you suspect fraud or misrepresentation in advertising, advise the NARB by letter; enclose a copy of the advertisement if possible. The agency will investigate or redirect your complaint.

Automobile Consumer Action Panel (AutoCAP). Contact information may be obtained from your library, courthouse, or the Center for Auto Safety, address below.

AutoCAP is a consumer-action panel composed of citizen laymen and members of the automobile industry. It will listen to your problem (verbal or written), make recommendations, and take action as warranted, either by panel, industry committee, or single mediator.

Local Consumer Organizations. Local organizations for consumers are usually staffed by local volunteers acting on consumer-interest issues. Not every area has one, but you can send details of your complaint to the Center for Auto Safety, 1223 Dupont Circle Building, Washington, D.C. 20036, which will forward your letter to the group nearest you.

ONE STEP BEYOND

Most dealerships do not want adverse publicity in newspapers or on the radio and television. Most areas have a consumer-action line or help line that works through a local mass-media communications system—television or radio. When it becomes necessary to solicit help from agencies, you might as well get everyone involved. If the problem is serious enough, you may even get a news camera crew and a reporter on the scene.

Nothing will rattle a dealership more than a well-organized picket. If possible, get others who have had a bad experience with your dealer to join your peaceful protest. Begin by learning local regulations regarding picketing and obtaining permission or a license to picket. Call the police chief or courthouse. Find out whether a license is necessary, and even if it is not, advise local law enforcement officials of your plans for a peaceful demonstration. Certain areas may restrict the size of your group and the hours you may walk. Print placards with three- or four-word slogans that sum up your protest—"SOLD ME (US) A LEMON," "SERVICE STINKS," "MERCHANDISE DEFECTIVE"—large enough to be read by passing motorists. Type a one-page summary of your problems with the dealership, itemizing what you bought and when, your problems with the car, how many times it went in for service, and the attitude (in your opinion) of the dealership and have photocopies made—fifty should do. Pass these out to customers entering the dealership, but do not force a copy on anyone. Customers have the right to come and go unmolested. Be prepared to march until you get the results you want—the service you deserve. Have at least one person walking during every legal hour; split the duty up among your group so no one person is marching all day long.

LEGAL STEPS

Some problems will absolutely have to go to court to be resolved, but it need not be expensive. Most areas have a Legal Aid Society or Legal Services Agency offering assistance to those within certain lower income ranges. For a small sum of money (it is not free), you are given the name of a participating attorney, an appointment is usually set for you to talk to him, and he will let you pour your heart out. He will then advise you of just what rights you have in the matter, the probability of going to court, what it will cost you to instigate legal proceedings, and your chances of walking away victorious. For the dollars invested in this way, it is well worth it just to find out where you stand legally, and what recourse you may or may not expect.

If your attorney advises you to file suit under the Magnuson-Moss Warranty Act, let the Federal Trade Commission know. Write to Warranties Project, Bureau of Consumer Protection, Federal Trade Commission, Washington, D.C. 20580.

Small claims court, found in every state, offers legal relief usually without the expense of an attorney, but there are limits that vary from state to state. Your local courthouse can advise you whether you fall within minimum/maximum dollar amounts and whether an attorney is required. The maximum ranges run from $300 to $3,000, and the waiting period for resolution runs from 3 weeks to 3 months. Again, the better your records, the better the results.

LETTERS

Any letter of complaint should be no more than one page in length, typewritten if possible, single-or double-spaced. When someone is holding two or three pages in his hand he has a tendency to scan the letter to pick out the important parts and read just enough to get the general drift of the material content. Keep it as simple as possible, but be thorough.

When you send a letter to a district office for action by a factory representative, explain the distribution: one copy to the district office, one copy to the manufacturer, one copy to the dealership. The manufacturer will then contact the district office, the district office will contact the dealership and/or you, and your problem should be on its way to a solution. Manufacturers normally send their dealers report cards monthly that state the number of complaints, the names of the complainants, and the nature of the complaints. Even so, the manufacturer allows the dealers a percentile factor of complaints before becoming really upset with a particular dealer. So do not send just one letter and expect miracles. Persistence pays.

SAMPLE FORM FOR COMPLAINT LETTER

On ————— I purchased a ————, serial number (——————),
(date)   (year, make)

from ——————————, located at ——————————————. The purchase
(dealership name)   address, city, state)

price was: —————.

These problems existed at the time I took delivery and were to be taken care of by the dealer (or his salesman).
(List the problems):
1.——————————————
2.——————————————

I have had the following problems since purchase and received service or lack of service on these dates:
(Itemize the problems and dates):
1.——————————————
2.——————————————

The service department has (choose one or all): failed to remedy the problems properly; created excessive and unnecessary delays; charged me for service rendered that was covered by warranty; been rude and discourteous; caused a great deal of worry and anxiety; used my car for errands; put excessive mileage on my car while it was in for service; misrepresented; broken promises; lied (or whatever else the dealer may have done to you personally).

Efforts to negotiate a settlement have failed. I have talked to: ———————— and ———————— and have received no satisfaction to date.

I want the following to resolve these problems: $————— cash

settlement; parts repaired/replaced; work done on the (engine, transmission, other); mediation to establish a fair settlement.

(If a warranty was issued in writing, enclose a photocopy with your correspondence. If a verbal warranty was given, detail the promises made. Include photocopies of anything you signed—contracts or agreements. The more complete your information, the better the results.)

MANUFACTURER CONTACT INFORMATION

American Motors Corporation, 14250 Plymouth Road, Detroit, Michigan 48232. Telephone: 313-493-2000.

Chrysler Corporation, 341 Massachusetts Avenue, Detroit, Michigan 48231. Telephone: 313-956-5252.

Ford Motor Company, The American Road, Dearborn, Michigan 48231. Telephone: 313-322-3000.

General Motors Corporation, 767 Fifth Avenue, New York, New York 10009. Telephone: 212-486-5000.

Chevrolet Motor Division, Div. General Motors, General Motors Building, Detroit, Michigan 48202. Telephone: 313-873-7200.

Pontiac Motor Division, Div. General Motors, One Pontiac Plaza, Pontiac, Michigan 48053. Telephone: 313-857-5000.

Oldsmobile Division, Div. General Motors, 920 Townsend Street, Lansing, Michigan 48921. Telephone: 517-373-5000.

Buick Motor Division, Div. General Motors, 902 E. Hamilton Avenue, Flint, Michigan 48550. Telephone: 313-766-5000.

Cadillac Motor Car Division, Div. General Motors, 2860 Clark Avenue, Detroit Michigan 48232. Telephone: 313-554-5147.

Import manufacturer contact information is available at your library.

The ball is in your lap. What you do in an individual situation is entirely up to you. If you choose to be docile about your problems and not to pursue a remedy to the end, it is you who must live with the results and suffer through the problems, and it is your responsibility to take actions necessary to obtain results. Never feel that a problem is too small to warrant remedial action. Never feel that since you made a mistake in judgment while buying your car that you must now live with that mistake. Never shake your head in resignation and say, "Well, they got me that time; but I'll know better next time." Dealerships rely upon these consumer attitudes to skirt the issue and take them out of the line of fire. Every time a consumer says, "Forget it; it is too insignificant or too late to pursue," the dealership cash register does a little jingle. Stand up for your rights and be persistent.

Best of luck to you.

Index